THE FRENCH COOK

Other books in The French Cook series:
Sauces
Soufflés (forthcoming)
Soups and Stews (forthcoming)

THE FRENCH COOK

CREAM PUFFS
& ÉCLAIRS

HOLLY HERRICK

Photographs by Alexandra DeFurio

GIBBS SMITH
TO ENRICH AND INSPIRE HUMANKIND

"Happily [choux] is one of the easiest pastries
to make: bring a little water and butter to a simmer in
a saucepan, dump in flour, beat over heat to thicken it,
and whip in a few eggs. That's all there is to it . . ."

–Julia Child, *The Way to Cook,* 1989

First Edition
13 14 15 16 17   10 9 8 7 6 5 4 3 2 1

Text © 2013 Holly Herrick
Photographs © 2013 Alexandra DeFurio

Published by
Gibbs Smith
P.O. Box 667
Layton, Utah 84041

1.800.835.4993 orders
www.gibbs-smith.com

Design by Sheryl Dickert
Page production by Melissa Dymock
Printed and bound in China

Gibbs Smith books are printed on either recycled, 100% post-consumer
waste, FSC-certified papers or on paper produced from sustainable PEFC-
certified forest/controlled wood source. Learn more at www.pefc.org.

Library of Congress Cataloging-in-Publication Data

Herrick, Holly.
The French cook : cream puffs & eclairs / Holly Herrick ;
photographs by Alexandra DeFurio. — First edition.
pages cm
title: Cream puffs & eclairs
Includes index.
ISBN 978-1-4236-3243-6
1. Cooking, French. 2. Pastry. 3. Confectionery. I. Title. II. Title: Cream puffs & eclairs.
TX719.H396 2013
641.5973—dc23
2013012904

To all French chefs everywhere, including my chefs
and mentors at Le Cordon Bleu, especially Jean
Claude Boucheret. *Merci a vous!* You all make the
world a more beautiful and delicious place.

Contents

Introduction

As a new bride in the 1990s, uprooted from New York to another state, I had time to indulge my interest in cooking, long-held since childhood and cooking with my nanna. Relying very heavily on *The Way to Cook,* by Julia Child, which had been a wedding present, I immersed myself into the wonderful world of (mostly) classical French cooking. I was quickly hooked, simmering, baking, saucing and roasting my way towards all kinds of new foods and pleasures.

The cooking itch soon became a passion, and that's just about when all of the really lucky confluences started happening. I decided to put my college journalism major to work not in general writing, but in food writing in particular. My mother-in-law, a marvelous cook and an ardent gourmand, went along with my husband and me to my first-ever food and wine festival in Aspen, Colorado. It was there that I saw Julia Child, my childhood idol, performing a demonstration in which she tackled a rather large steamed lobster with a huge mallet. I summoned the nerve to approach Julia and ask what she thought I should do to get qualified as a food writer. Her graceful answer was actually more of a question: "Can you get to Le Cordon Bleu in Paris?"

I practically squealed *oui!* As good fortune would have it, my husband supported me on this quest. Many years of having studied French and functioning as a sort of uninitiated Francophile practically carried me over the ocean to Paris. Upon landing, a sense of clarity and purpose hit me in a flash, even as I saw the little rabbits scurrying around the fields surrounding Charles de Gaulle airport. I was home, and it felt *delicieux.*

Since then, I've worked in many kitchens and traveled all over the world, but nothing has touched me like my French experience.

It's an honor to be the author of this second volume in The French Cook series.

A Few Words on Choux Pastry

Mon petit choux (my little cabbage) is a common term of endearment in France, not unlike "my darling" or "my dear" in English. Similarly, choux pastry is a much beloved and ultra-versatile pastry that is truly unlike any other. Where most pastries—such as a short pastry used in tarts—rely on minimal gluten activation to maximize crispiness and tenderness, choux pastry likes to get beat up a bit with a wooden spoon. This actually maximizes gluten and helps create the light, airy, moist interior and crispy exterior crunch for which choux is so celebrated.

Like many culinary wonders and other French classics such as the *tarte tatin*, choux is thought to have originated as something of a mistake. The popular theory is that an errant pastry chef whipped up a pastry cream (usually a sweet pastry filling), forgot to add the sugar, and baked it, yielding something very similar to what we now know as choux.

Indeed, barring the sugar, the ingredients in a pastry cream (page 66) and choux pastry are quite similar. Choux begins by beating flour into warm water and melted butter to form a thick white dough. Eggs are then added gradually until a glossy, smooth, beautiful pastry dough is formed. The gluten in the flour provides the structure, the butter gives it flavor and depth, and the eggs encourage the glorious lift and puff of the choux.

It's not a complicated pastry. In fact, at Le Cordon Bleu in Paris, where I first prepared it, choux was part of the beginning cuisine curriculum. We'll go into more detail about preparing the pastry itself in The Art of Making Choux Pastry (page 15), but for now, what matters is to contemplate the virtually endless possibilities for choux pastry. Because the slightly nutty, buttery flavor is neutral, the puffy shapes so pretty and appealing, and the texture both elegant and homey, choux can become the casing for many wonderful sweet or savory treats of all shapes and sizes.

Pâte à choux blended with grated cheese and possibly some fresh herbs becomes a warm, inviting cheese puff to have with a sip of Champagne before dinner. Or, filled with ham and cheese, the same puff can become a satisfying, elegant sandwich for lunch or to serve at cocktail parties. You can fill choux pastries with warm sautéed onions topped with cheese, a blend of cheese and smoked salmon and caviar, or roast beef and a horseradish cream—anything goes! *Tout est possible* (the sky is the limit). But don't stop there. Add a bit of sugar to the flour and you have a slightly sweetened choux, the base for myriad sweet concoctions such as éclairs, St. Honoré, croquembouche, cream puffs and more filled with glorious butter creams, whipped creams, puddings, and ice creams paired with sauces and glazes of infinite varieties. Fried choux becomes a *beignet*, or French doughnut.

This book is divided into two parts: savory and sweet. Like most meals, it begins with the savory (pages 27–59) and ends with the sweet desserts (pages 60–109). Along the way, there will be all kinds of tips and beautiful photography to help make your choux adventure as enjoyable and delicious as can be.

Bon appetit!

cinnamon sugar

orange sugar

Maple salt

L'Art de la Pâte à Choux
The Art of Making Choux Pastry

Demystifying the Puff

Before you get started, it is very important and liberating to breathe deeply and remember that pâte à choux is an extremely easy, forgiving and flexible pastry. The simplicity begins with the ingredients: water, salt, (a little sugar for sweet pastry), butter, flour and eggs. The water can come straight from the tap. I recommend using kosher salt or sea salt because of its nonchemical flavor, but any will do if it's what you have on hand. Butter should be unsalted and cool for easier handling, as it is cut into cubes before being added to the water.

The type of flour to use is something of a debate in pastry circles and it all goes back to the protein content. Remember, choux likes high gluten content, and the higher the protein content of the flour, the higher the gluten content of the pastry. For this book, I tested many combinations of flours and got the best results using equal parts bread flour (about 14–16 percent protein) and all-purpose flour (about 10–12 percent protein), so that's what I suggest in the master recipes, both savory and sweet, page 28 and 62 respectively). However, if you have only one or the other flour at home

on the day you decide to make choux, you should have good results using either, so don't fret.

As for the eggs, use the freshest available and add them to the pastry at room temperature, if possible. In most cases, to maximize sheen and color, an egg wash will be brushed over the top of the pastry just before it goes into the oven.

Because preparing choux goes quickly, you will want to have everything ready before you actually start cooking: preheat the oven, line the baking sheets (see Equipment for Preparing Choux Pastry, page 23), measure the ingredients and sift the dry ingredients, prepare the pastry bag with a fitted tip, and have the beaten egg wash on standby.

Choux is a great pastry to make ahead in several batches, because it's easily stored (once cool) overnight in an airtight container or for several weeks in the freezer in a plastic bag. While the choux bakes, there is time to clean up the kitchen and prepare for rounds 2, 3, 4 or more. While you may be tempted to double or triple the master recipes, I don't recommend it. Working with that much quantity gets unwieldy and will deliver sub-par results, not to mention one very tired stirring arm. Better to prepare the pastry in multiple batches, then you have it on hand when you need it. It takes just minutes to whip up a filling (in most cases) and fill the choux, and voilà—entertaining made easy.

MAKING CHOUX THE RIGHT WAY

Bring the water, butter and salt to a gentle simmer in a medium, straight-sided, heavy-bottom saucepan over medium-high heat. Once the butter has completely melted, add the sifted flour and salt (plus sugar for sweet pastry) all at once to the water mixture. Immediately incorporate the flour by stirring vigorously with a good, old-fashioned wooden spoon. Reduce the heat to medium. The flour and water mixture will merge almost at once to form a fairly tight ball. The "mixture" will be the color of milk and its texture slightly reminiscent of a freshly opened can of Play-Doh. Keep stirring the pastry ball until it pulls away from the sides of the pan and the bottom is mostly clear of pastry. This whole process should take almost exactly 1 minute. It is important to "dry out" the dough through this process so it will be ready to accept the eggs, which will encourage lift in the oven.

Remove the pan from the stove and set it aside on your work surface. Allow the dough to cool for about 30 seconds to 1 minute, stirring occasionally, until it is cool enough to comfortably touch with your fingertip for 10 seconds. (If the pastry is too hot when the eggs are added, things can get messy fast.)

For the master pastry recipes provided in this book, I use a total of 1 cup of eggs (roughly 4 large eggs beaten together). From here, the task is to incorporate the eggs into the pastry, and it's probably the oddest-looking leg of the journey, at least initially. Add half of the egg mixture all at once to the pastry. Stir vigorously with a wooden spoon. (Some prefer using a blender or mixer to incorporate the eggs, but I feel it is unnecessary and tends to require extra cleanup.) At first, the dough will look like the eggs have no intention of merging with the flour mixture. But after a minute of stirring, the eggs suddenly and almost miraculously "take" to the mixture, and it becomes smooth and glossy. From here, add the remaining eggs in two equal parts ($1/4$ cup each) and repeat as before. The final pastry should be golden yellow, glossy and smooth, and yield to the touch. It is best to pipe it onto your baking sheet while it is still warm and fresh from the pan (unless you plan to refrigerate it for later use). So, get ready to go!

Melting butter in the water

Stirring in the flour

Stirring eggs into the dough

Finished choux dough, ready for baking

PIPING AND SCOOPING
Shaping Your Choux

As lovely as warm choux is to look at, it is messy to the touch if not properly managed. If you're like me, and have a mild aversion to pastry bags and pastry tips, you will find that these tools, for the most part (with the exception of spoon-plopping choux into balls; see page 19), are your allies when making choux. There are two reasons: it prevents the need to touch the sticky pastry with your hands, and it neatly shapes the pastry into consistent shapes. I recommend 12-inch disposable plastic bags, because this size neatly manages dough for piping two rounds (half the batch in each) of the master recipes in this book, and cleaning up means throwing the bags away instead of enduring the frustration of trying to wash them clean, which is no small matter.

The size of the pastry tip matters, too. For forming all the shapes in this book, I use my trusted #806 round, stainless steel pastry tip. The size and shape of the desired choux is simply manipulated by the amount of pressure put on the bag and the direction you lead it when piping. To fit the bag with the #806 round tip, cut off about 1 inch from the bottom of the bag. Press the tip firmly into the opening so that it fits tightly. Holding the bag in your favored working hand (I'm right-handed, so I hold the bag with my left and fill it with the spatula in my right hand), roll the bag down about one-quarter of its length over your "holding" hand to form a sleeve. With a medium spatula, scoop the warm pastry into the bag. When it's about three-quarters full, pull the sleeve up, squeeze the pastry slightly to pop any air pockets (some pastry may escape through the tip; this is okay), and roll the top

of the bag over itself to seal the pastry neatly in the bag. Now you're ready to pipe!

No matter what size you're about to pipe, all choux needs to land on a baking sheet that is lined with either a silicon mat or parchment paper (see Equipment for Preparing Choux Pastry, page 23). Do not butter or grease the sheets, as it will result in a slippery mess. Have a small bowl of cool water handy and be ready to gently press down any slight twirls or bumps with a wet fingertip. Brush each pastry lightly with egg wash before moving to the oven. Separate the oven racks to encourage air circulation and allow room for the choux to puff, with one at the bottom of the oven and the other in the middle.

Freshly piped dough. The next steps are to press down the tip with a dampened fingertip, brush with egg wash and bake.

Piping Size How-To

Piping Petits Choux
(small, 1-inch balls)

Hold the pastry tip/bag at an angle, with the tip pressing lightly onto the lined baking sheet. Work horizontally from one side of the sheet to the other, spacing 1 to 2 inches between balls. Squeeze the bag gently to form 1-inch-diameter choux, about $1/2$ inch high.

Or, to form with a spoon, dip the spoon in water (this prevents dough from sticking to the spoon), collect 1 tablespoon of dough onto the spoon and then drop it off the spoon, spacing at 1- to 2-inch intervals. Continue to dip and drop for each choux until it's gone.

Piping Gros Choux
(large, 2-inch balls)

Hold the pastry tip/bag at an angle, with the tip pressing lightly onto the lined baking sheet. Work horizontally from one side of the sheet to the other, spacing 2 inches between balls. Squeeze the bag gently to form 2-inch-diameter choux, about 1 inch high.

Or, to form with a spoon, dip the spoon in water, collect 2 tablespoons of pastry dough and then drop it off the spoon, spacing at 2-inch intervals.

Piping Petits Éclairs
(small, $2^1/2$-inch-long éclairs)

Hold the pastry tip/bag at an angle, with the tip pressing lightly onto the lined baking sheet. Work horizontally from one side of the sheet to the other, spacing 2 inches between lengths of dough. Squeeze the bag gently to form éclairs $2^1/4$ inches long, about $1/2$ inch high and $1/2$ inch wide.

Piping Gros Éclairs
(large, 4-inch-long éclairs)

Hold the pastry tip/bag at an angle, with the tip pressing lightly onto the lined baking sheet. Work horizontally from one side of the sheet to the other, spacing 2 inches between lengths of dough. Squeeze the bag gently to form éclairs $3^1/2$ inches long, about $3/4$ inch high and 1 inch wide.

Piping Petits Ronds
(small, 4-inch-diameter rings)

Hold the pastry tip/bag at an angle, with the tip pressing lightly onto the lined baking sheet. Work horizontally from one side of the sheet to the other, spacing 2 inches between rings. Aim for consistency in size by using your eyes. If desired, it's possible to outline a 4-inch ring with a pencil on the underside of parchment paper or on the silicon mat as a guide. This may be the best approach for beginning pastry pipers and perfectionists; otherwise, just pipe free-form. Beginning at the "top" of the circle, pipe, squeezing the bag gently to form 4-inch-diameter rings, $1/2$ inch high and $1/2$ inch wide. Continue with a second, slightly narrower layer on top of the base layer.

Piping Gros Ronds
(large, 14-inch-diameter rings)

As with the small rings, it's helpful to guide the size and shape of the ring by outlining a circle (you can use a pot or a pot lid of about this size) in pencil on the underside of parchment paper or on the silicon mat before you pipe. Hold the pastry tip/bag at an angle, with the tip pressing lightly onto the lined baking sheet. Beginning at the "top" of the circle, squeeze out a 14-inch circle, about 1 inch wide and $1/2$ inch high. Top that with another layer of dough, following the same directions. If there is still dough left, repeat with a third layer.

BAKING AND FILLING

Quantities yielded from the master recipes (pages 28 and 62) and cooking times vary for different sizes of choux, of course, and are indicated with each recipe throughout the book.

Regardless of the cooking time, the end result should be a puffy, deep golden, slightly shiny crust with somewhat irregular heights. The sides should be firm and hold their shape. Inside, the pastry should be soft yet firm to the touch, almost like an omelet. The internal network of air pocket casings should be supple but firm and moist. (This is the stuff of choux dreams, and you'll soon be spinning your own.)

Once done baking, turn off the oven and leave the door open about 5 minutes to allow the choux to dry a little bit further before transferring them to a pastry rack to cool. When cool enough to handle, pierce the bottom of each choux with the tip of a small, sharp paring knife to allow for steam to escape. Dry thoroughly on cooling racks before filling and serving. Optionally, store dry pastries in an airtight container overnight. Choux also freezes very well. Once cool, arrange the pastries gently in a freezer bag, without crowding. Freeze for up to 1 month. Before filling, bring to room temperature and refresh or "crisp" for about 5 minutes in a 350°F oven. Allow to cool before filling.

What filling goes in each choux size and shape, and the method for filling varies considerably between sweet and savory varieties. For example, a sweet éclair's "hidden" filling will be piped through a series of small holes at the bottom, while a savory éclair, served more like a sandwich, will be sliced and filled. Also, a sweet éclair or choux is often finished with a glaze or powdered sugar and a sauce. Each recipe in this book includes filling suggestions and instructions.

As you work through the recipes in the book and hopefully play with your own ideas for flavor combinations, always consider what filling makes sense for the particular size and shape of choux with which you are working. For instance, a petit savory choux should be paired with flavors, textures, and quantities that complement it without overwhelming it. One of my favorite examples of a well-matched filling and shape in this book are the savory Small Éclairs with Avocado Mousse, Bacon and Tomatoes (page 52). A pretty and fun riff on the classic BLT, the soft, bright green guacamole bed is the ideal foil for crunchy bites of bacon and tender tomatoes that top it. The longer shape helps reveal the filling and also makes eating and enjoying this particular éclair easier. There are many, many delicious examples, both sweet and savory, all along the way.

Amusez-vous bien!

Halved petits choux

Piping in the filling

Ready to top and serve

La Batterie de Cuisine pour la Preparation de la Pâte à Choux
Equipment for Preparing Choux Pastry

For the Choux Pastry

Saucepan: A sturdy, straight-sided saucepan with a heavy bottom (preferably copper interior) is needed to facilitate enough movement of the pastry for stirring together the water, butter and flour and drying it out sufficiently. I recommend a 4-quart, straight-sided saucepan.

Wooden spoon: A standard-size wooden spoon (without a hole in the center) is the best tool for incorporating the flour and the eggs into the pastry.

Medium-size nonreactive bowl: This works nicely for turning out the dough for cooling slightly before incorporating the eggs.

Half-sheet baking pans: You will want at least two in your kitchen—good-quality aluminum 13 x 18-inch pans, preferably with 1-inch-high sides to prevent losing a choux or two off the edges of the sheet when you're moving it around.

Silicon baking mats and/or parchment paper: Both provide easy solutions for keeping the choux from sticking to the baking sheet. A recent convert to the reusable and easy-to-clean-and-store silicon mats (I recommend the French SilPat brand), I also like the ease and availability of parchment paper. The silicon mats come pre-sized for half-sheet baking pans, which is much easier than fussing with sizing the parchment paper. You will want at least two of the half-sheet-size ($11^5/8$ x $16^1/2$-inch) silicon mats if you decide to go that route (two mats accommodate one batch of the choux master recipes in this book). They're inexpensive, last forever when properly cared for, and roll nicely for easy storage.

Pastry bag(s): Recommended not just for piping the pastry but also for filling some of the recipes in this book. I like the sturdy nature of Ateco brand 12-inch disposable plastic bags. A reusable pastry bag is also an alternative, but use at least a 12-inch size for easiest handling. Bags that are much bigger can get a little unwieldy.

Pastry tips: It's worth your while to own a set of assorted tips (I recommend Ateco's 12-tip set).

Pastry brush: A small or medium pastry brush will be needed to brush down the choux with egg wash before baking. Natural bristle brushes do the best job of spreading the wash without dripping, but some of the plastic and other varieties are fine, too. Buy the best quality you can afford. Wash gently in hot, soapy water and dry thoroughly to help your brush last as long as possible.

FOR THE FILLINGS, GLAZES, SAUCES, ETC.

Whisk: An easy way to mount cream, meringues, and more without plugging in any machinery is to use a whisk and old-fashioned arm power. A medium-size whisk can handle almost any job for the home cook.

Saucepans: A medium and small saucepan will be needed for preparing sweet sauces such as ganache, crème anglaise and many more.

Chinois or mesh strainer: Helpful for straining out any clumps or unsavory bits of cooked egg or other unwanted sauce residuals.

Stacked mixing bowls: An added bonus in any kitchen and handy for preparing whipped cream, butter cream and other choux fillings. A variety of sizes—small, medium, large and very large—is ideal.

Good-quality knives: All kitchens should be equipped with at least a paring knife and an 8- to12-inch chef's knife for chopping, slicing and dicing anything from chocolate to onions and everything in between.

Hand-held mixer or stand mixer: Though not mandatory, it's helpful to have an electric mixer on hand, especially for mounting and blending larger quantities of fillings.

Ice cream maker: There are several recipes for homemade ice cream in this book. An electric machine, with its constant speed and temperature regulation, makes for the creamiest of ice creams. However, ice cream can be stirred (see Hot Tips for Ice Cream, page 87) from time to time as it is setting, to fairly closely simulate the action of an electric ice cream maker. If making ice cream is not your thing, you can always substitute a near flavor substitute with one of the many top-quality commercial ice creams.

CHAPTER 1

LES CHOUX À LA CRÈME SAVOUREUSE
Savory Cream Puffs and Choux Rings

Whether piped into petites choux and filled with salmon and cream cheese or onion confit and melted cheese; simmered like pasta in water to form fragrant, savory choux gnocchi; or rolled out as toppers for individual pot pies, choux flexes its versatility muscle in all kinds of delicious ways in this chapter. For round choux balls, piping is not required if you choose to go the old-fashioned spoon route. Just have two teaspoons (for small choux) or two tablespoons (for large choux) nearby in a glass of cold water. Dip the spoons in the water and grab a heaping spoon of the dough in one spoon, using the other to help shape it into a neat round. Drop onto the prepared sheet, brush with egg wash and bake.

RECETTE MAÎTRESSE POUR LA PÂTE À CHOUX SAVOUREUX

Master Recipe for Savory Cream Puffs
(for preparing savory choux puffs, éclairs and rings)

(YIELDS 24 TO 30 PETITS CHOUX, 12 TO 14 GROS CHOUX, 26 TO 30 PETITS ÉCLAIRS, 12 GROS ÉCLAIRS, 6 PETITS RINGS, 1 GROS RING)

For a detailed description of the choux pastry preparation process, see "De-Mystifying the Puff" (page 15) and "Making Choux the Right Way" (page 16). This recipe provides the ingredient quantities and a more abbreviated description.

1 cup water

3/4 stick (3 ounces) cold unsalted butter cut into
   1/2-inch cubes

1/2 cup bread flour

1/2 cup all-purpose flour

1/2 teaspoon sea salt or kosher salt

4 large eggs (about 1 cup), room temperature,
   beaten together

Egg wash: 1 egg yolk, splash of water, pinch of salt,
   blended together

Preheat the oven according to specific recipe instructions that follow in this book (temperatures will vary according to choux size). Line two half-sheet baking pans with silicon mats or parchment paper. Measure all the ingredients and have them ready before starting to prepare the choux dough.

In a medium, heavy-bottom saucepan, heat the water and butter together over medium-high heat, stirring once or twice to help the butter melt. Then reduce the heat to medium.

Sift together the two flours and salt over a medium bowl. Add the sifted dry ingredients all at once to the butter and water mixture, and set the bowl nearby. Stir the mixture vigorously with a wooden spoon to help bring it into one cohesive ball. Continue stirring, less vigorously, until the pastry pulls away from the sides of the pan, another minute or so. Turn the dough out into the reserved bowl and let sit for about 1 minute, or until the pastry is cool enough to touch comfortably with your fingertip for at least 10 seconds. Add half of the beaten eggs (about 1/2 cup) to the pastry. Stir vigorously with a wooden spoon until the dough looks uniform and glossy, about 1 minute. Add half of the remaining egg mixture (about 1/4 cup) and continue to stir until the dough is uniform and glossy, about 1 minute. Repeat with the remaining egg mixture.

While the dough is still warm, pipe and bake according to specific recipe directions. (For a more detailed overview, see "Piping and Scooping," page 18 and "Piping Size How-To," page 19.) Brush the top of each pastry with a light coating of egg wash, being careful not to let the wash drip down the sides.

"Soupe" à l'Oignon aux Petits Choux de Gruyère Fondu

French Onion "Soup" with Melted Gruyère Cheese in Savory Cream Puffs

(YIELDS 24 TO 30 PETITS CHOUX)

All the elements of the classic French onion soup—caramelized onion, wine, thyme, beef stock, and melted, nutty Gruyère cheese—come together in warm, satisfying bites, each encased with delicate choux pastry. Perfect for a winter cocktail party or as an aperitif before any meal, these will quickly become a classic in your home. Make the choux and the fillings ahead of time if you like; then re-crisp the pastry, reheat the filling and assemble in minutes for a fuss-free flavor event.

1 Master Recipe Savory Choux Pastry (page 28)

Egg wash: 1 egg yolk, splash of water, pinch of salt, blended together

For the filling:

2 tablespoons unsalted butter

1 tablespoon olive oil

1 large sweet onion, finely diced (about 3 cups)

1 large shallot, finely diced (about 1/4 cup)

Dash of sea salt or kosher salt

Freshly ground black pepper

3 large cloves garlic, very finely chopped

3 tablespoons white wine (e.g., Chardonnay)

1/2 teaspoon concentrated beef stock or 1/2 cup standard beef stock

1/4 teaspoon honey

1 teaspoon chopped fresh thyme leaves

1 cup grated Gruyère or Swiss cheese

Preheat oven to 425°F.

Prepare Savory Choux Pastry. Pipe onto lined baking sheets according to "Piping Size How-To" for small choux (page 19). Brush each choux lightly with egg wash and bake for 20 to 25 minutes, or until puffed and golden brown. Turn off the oven, open the door, and let the pastry stand for 5 minutes. Then remove from oven and close door; turn heat to 400°F. Transfer choux to a pastry rack. When cool enough to handle, pierce the bottom of each gently with the tip of a knife, and cool completely on a the rack.

Meanwhile, prepare the filling. Melt the butter and olive oil together in a large sauté pan over medium heat. Add the onion and shallot and season lightly with salt and pepper. Cook, stirring to coat, for 5 minutes, or until softened. Add the garlic and cook another few minutes. Increase

continued >

heat to medium-high and add the wine and stock. Cook until almost all of the liquid has reduced, about 3 minutes. Add the honey and thyme. Cook through to heat. Taste and adjust seasonings as needed. Reserve warm.

To assemble, gently cut through the center of each choux (horizontally) using a sharp or serrated knife. Reserve the tops separately. Fill each choux bottom with 1 teaspoon onion mixture and top with about 1 teaspoon grated cheese. Place the filled choux bottoms on a baking sheet and heat in the preheated oven until the cheese is melted and bubbling, about 5 minutes. Cap each choux with the reserved tops. Serve immediately on a platter, garnished with a few sprigs of fresh thyme.

PETITS CHOUX AUX EPINARDS CRÉMEUX ET CROQUANTS
Small Savory Cream Puffs with Crunchy Creamed Spinach

(YIELDS 24 TO 30 PETITS CHOUX)

Jewel-toned spinach gets infused with a generous dash of pungent nutmeg and the soothing taste of whole cream in this beautiful and impossible-to-resist taste treat. The crunch of finely chopped water chestnuts is an idyllic foil to the creamy, warm blend inside its crunchy choux casing. Frozen spinach saves time and, usually, money. This filling comes together quickly and goes just as fast. Assemble just before serving.

1 Master Recipe Savory Choux Pastry (page 28)
Egg wash: 1 egg yolk, splash of water, pinch of salt, blended together

For the filling:
1 (10- ounce) package frozen leaf spinach
2 tablespoons unsalted butter
1/2 small onion, finely diced (about 3/4 cup)

Dash of sea salt or kosher salt
Freshly ground black pepper
1/2 cup finely chopped water chestnuts
2 teaspoons Champagne vinegar (or 1 teaspoon white wine or cider vinegar)
1/4 teaspoon ground nutmeg
1/2 cup heavy cream
1/3 cup grated aged Parmesan cheese

Preheat oven to 425°F.

Prepare Savory Choux Pastry. Pipe onto lined baking sheets according to "Piping Size How-To" for small choux (page 19). Brush each choux lightly with egg wash and bake for 20 to 25 minutes, or until puffed and golden brown. Turn off the oven, open the door, and let the pastry stand for 5 minutes. Then remove from oven, transfer to a cooling rack, and when cool enough to handle, pierce the bottom of each choux gently with the tip of a knife. Let cool completely.

Meanwhile, prepare the filling. Thaw the spinach in the microwave or in a small pan according to package directions.

Heat the butter in a large sauté pan over medium-high heat. Add the onion, season lightly with salt and pepper, and sauté for 5 minutes, or until just softened.

Turn out the thawed spinach into a clean kitchen towel; twist the ends of the towel around the spinach and twist over the sink, discarding any excess juice. Reduce the sauté pan to medium heat. Chop the spinach finely and add to the sautéed onions. Stir and heat through about 5 minutes. Add the water chestnuts, vinegar and nutmeg. Cook a few minutes, until the vinegar has evaporated. Stir in the cream and Parmesan cheese. Taste and adjust seasonings as needed. Reserve warm. (*Note:* The filling can be made a day or two ahead, refrigerated covered, and reheated just before filling the choux and serving.)

To assemble, gently cut through the center of each choux (horizontally) using a sharp or serrated knife, stopping just short of the other side, leaving the cap attached. Gently fill the bottom half of each choux with 1 scant teaspoon of the warm spinach filling. Serve warm.

Gougères aux Trois Fromages et au Poivre
Cheese Puffs with Three Cheeses and Pepper

(YIELDS 24 TO 30 PETITE CHOUX, OR 12 TO 14 GROS CHOUX)

Few things in life can beat a warm, crunchy cheese puff (known as gougère *in France) fresh out of the oven. This recipe includes a bit of freshly ground black pepper for kick (optional) and a combination of aged white cheddar, Gruyère and Parmesan cheeses blended into the warm choux and melted just before piping and baking. I serve them as a warm variation on bread alongside a green salad to start a meal. Especially sturdy because of the cheese, these puffs freeze very well and reheat in a snap for instant entertaining.*

1 Master Recipe Savory Choux Pastry (page 28)
1 teaspoon ground black pepper
1/2 cup grated aged white cheddar cheese
1/2 cup grated Gruyère or Swiss cheese

3 tablespoons grated Parmesan cheese
Egg wash: 1 egg yolk, splash of water, pinch of salt,
   blended together

Preheat oven to 425°F.

Prepare Savory Choux Pastry. While still warm, stir in the ground pepper, cheddar, Gruyère and Parmesan. Blend with a wooden spoon until just melted. Pipe onto lined baking sheets according to "Piping Size How-To" for small choux (page 19) or, if desired, for large choux (page 19). Brush each choux lightly with egg wash. Bake the small choux for 20 to 25 minutes, and the large choux for 35 minutes, or until puffed and golden brown. Turn off the oven, open the door, and let the pastry stand for 5 minutes. Then remove from oven, transfer to a cooling rack, and when cool enough to handle, pierce the bottom of each choux gently with the tip of a knife. Let cool completely.

Variations: Sprinkle the warm petits choux with freshly chopped chives or another fresh herb, such as rosemary. Or, for cheese puff sandwiches, halve horizontally and fill with a dollop of mayonnaise and small spears of roasted asparagus, fresh arugula tossed with a bit of lemon juice and olive oil, or a layer of crisp bacon and thinly sliced tomato.

Petits Pots de Fruits de Mer aux Choux
Seafood Pot Pies

(YIELDS 6 INDIVIDUAL POT PIES)

Choux makes an outstanding replacement for puff pastry or short pastry for pot pies. Leek, fennel, a splash of orange juice, Pernod, and a pinch of saffron make zesty flavor companions for sexy lobster and salmon. The base for the pot pies can be made a day ahead and refrigerated. Preheat the oven and prepare the pastry just before they're ready to bake in the oven. Serve these babies hot from the oven. The choux will absorb the liquid from the sauce if it's left to linger too long. There is little risk of that happening once the first spoon breaks the surface—these are that delicious and beautiful!

For the filling:

3 tablespoons butter

1 small onion, finely diced (about $^2/_3$ cup)

1 leek, green tops and base removed, quartered,
   well rinsed and finely chopped (about $1^3/_4$ cup)

1 large fennel bulb, halved, cored and finely diced
   (about 2 cups)

Sea salt or kosher salt

Ground white pepper

1 teaspoon fennel seeds

$^1/_4$ teaspoon saffron threads

1 tablespoon all-purpose flour

$1^1/_2$ cups clam juice or fish stock

3 tablespoons fresh-squeezed orange juice

1 teaspoon orange zest

2 teaspoons Pernod or another licorice liquor

$^1/_2$ cup half & half

1 cup frozen peas

$^3/_4$ cup shelled fresh, raw lobster tail meat cut into
   $^1/_2$-inch dice

$1^1/_4$ pounds fresh salmon filet, skin removed and
   cut into 1-inch dice

For the topping:

1 Master Recipe Savory Choux Pastry (page 28)

Egg wash: 1 egg yolk, splash of water, pinch of salt,
   blended together

Begin by preparing the filling, up to one day ahead. Arrange six $1^1/_2$-cup ramekins or ovenproof bowls on a baking sheet.

In a large saucepan, melt the butter over medium heat. Add the onion, leek, fennel, and a light pinch of salt and pepper; stir. Cook until softened, about 5 minutes. Add the fennel seeds and saffron, stir, and cook another minute. Sprinkle in the flour and stir to coat and cook through, 1 more minute. Add the clam juice or stock, then increase heat to high, stirring vigorously to incorporate. Add the orange juice, orange zest, and Pernod. Reduce heat to medium and cook together for 1 more minute.

Stir in the half & half and cook until the sauce is thick enough to coat the back of the wooden spoon. Remove mixture from the heat. Stir in the frozen peas. Taste and adjust seasonings as needed. Set aside for 5 minutes to cool slightly. Gently stir in the lobster and salmon. Using a large spoon, transfer the filling to the ramekins or bowls. Cover tightly with plastic wrap and refrigerate for at least 2 hours and up to 24 hours before finishing.

To finish, remove ramekins from the refrigerator and let come to room temperature while making the choux dough.

Preheat oven to 425°F. Prepare Savory Choux Pastry. Pipe three balls sized for small choux (see "Piping Size How-To," page 19), sides touching in a triangle, over the top of each filling. Brush choux lightly with egg wash and bake for 25 minutes, or until puffed and golden brown. Serve immediately.

Gnocchi de Pâte à Choux aux Fines Herbes, Sauce d'Echalotes et de Safran au Beurre

Herbed Savory Cream Puff Gnocchi with a Shallot and Saffron Butter Sauce

(YIELDS 10 GENEROUS APPETIZER PORTIONS, OR 4 TO 6 ENTRÉES)

Infinitely less complicated than making traditional gnocchi, piping choux directly into simmering (but not boiling), well-salted water yields little logs of tender, gnocchi-like dumplings. They take just the time of preparing the choux plus 20 to 25 minutes to cook. After the choux hit the water, they drop to the bottom and then pop to the top. A few more minutes of fattening and plumping up, and they're ready to drain, toss with seasoned butter and serve. The ease and bubbling drama of the preparation make it perfect for a dinner party or an evening of casual dining with friends or family. Kids will love them! If you're not a big fan of saffron, just leave it out. These need to be served fairly quickly but can be kept warm in the cooking water, off the heat, for 15 to 20 minutes.

For the choux gnocchi:

1 Master Recipe Savory Choux Pastry (page 28)

3 tablespoons finely ground cornmeal

1/4 cup finely chopped fresh chives

1/4 cup finely chopped fresh parsley leaves

1 tablespoon finely chopped fresh thyme leaves

Zest of 1 lemon

For the butter sauce:

1 stick (8 tablespoons) unsalted butter, cut into large cubes

1 small shallot, finely chopped

1/4 teaspoon saffron threads (optional)

Juice of 1/2 lemon

Sea salt or kosher salt

Freshly ground black pepper

Before starting the pastry, have a large pot of well-salted water on a very low simmer. Fit a pastry bag with the #806 round tip and have the ingredients measured and ready.

Prepare the Savory Choux Pastry, adding the cornmeal to the flour and salt before sifting. When the dough is cooked and still warm, stir in the chives, parsley, thyme and lemon zest with a wooden spoon.

Fill the prepared pastry bag with half of the dough. Pipe the dough over the simmering water

continued >

into $1/2$ to $3/4$-inch lengths, about $1/2$ inch thick, cutting off each portion with a kitchen scissor or paring knife to "plop" it into the water. Continue piping until the pastry bag is empty. The choux dumplings will rise to the surface after about 3 to 4 minutes, and will continue to plump and cook another 6 to 8 minutes, or until set. Drain with a slotted spoon onto a clean baking sheet lined with a cotton or linen towel. Fill the pastry bag with the remaining dough and repeat with the second batch.

Meanwhile, in a small saucepan, combine the butter, shallot, saffron, lemon juice and seasonings. Melt over medium heat, then reduce to low. Reserve warm over low heat.

To serve, arrange the gnocchi on individual plates and drizzle with a generous amount of the seasoned butter sauce. Or, serve on a platter and pass family style.

GNOCCHI DE PÂTE
À CHOUX GRATINÉS
Gratin of Savory Choux Gnocchi

(YIELDS 8 SIDE-DISH PORTIONS)

The same choux gnocchi, dressed with Parmesan and butter and baked in a hot oven, yields a cheesy, pasta-like delight that is perfect with roasted chicken, pork or a juicy steak. Simply poach the gnocchi as in the previous recipe and arrange the cooked, drained gnocchi in a large baking pan. Top with 1 cup grated Parmesan cheese and a couple pats of butter. Bake at 400°F for 20 minutes, or until golden and bubbling. Serve immediately.

Petites Choux au Saumon Fumé et aux Concombres
Small Savory Cream Puffs with Smoked Salmon and Cucumbers

(YIELDS 24 TO 30 PETITS CHOUX)

The rosy pink edges of smoked salmon dot an airy blend of cream cheese and sour cream seasoned with fresh dill and lemon to form the center of these elegant appetizers. A crisp, ultra-thin layer of cucumber forms the filling base, adding a pleasant and surprising crunch in each bite. If you can find one, use a mild, slender hothouse (also known as European) cucumber; leave the skin on for extra color and flavor. If using a fresh garden-variety cucumber, remove the bitter skin before slicing. Select a cucumber that closely matches the diameter of the baked choux, about 1 1/2 inches. Assemble these just before serving, but feel free to prep the fillings and choux puffs in advance.

1 Master Recipe Savory Choux Pastry (page 28)

Egg wash: 1 egg yolk, splash of water, pinch of salt, blended together

For the filling:

1/2 cup cream cheese, room temperature

1/2 cup sour cream

1/3 cup finely diced smoked salmon

1 tablespoon finely chopped dill fronds

1 teaspoon lemon zest

Dash of sea salt or kosher salt

Freshly ground black pepper

1/2 hothouse (a.k.a. European) cucumber, very thinly sliced, about 30 slices

Preheat oven to 425°F.

Prepare Savory Choux Pastry. Pipe onto lined baking sheets according to "Piping Size How-To" for small choux (page 19). Brush each choux lightly with egg wash and bake for 20 to 25 minutes, or until puffed and golden brown. Turn off the oven, open the door, and let the pastry stand for 5 minutes. Then remove from oven, transfer to a cooling rack, and when cool enough to handle, pierce the bottom of each choux gently with the tip of a knife. Let cool completely.

Meanwhile, in a medium bowl, whisk together the cream cheese and sour cream until well blended and fluffy. Fold in the salmon, dill and lemon zest. Season lightly to taste with salt (remember, the salmon is salty, so you won't need much) and pepper.

To assemble, gently cut through the center of each choux (horizontally) using a sharp or serrated knife, stopping just short of the other side, leaving the cap attached. Line the bottom of each choux with a slice of cucumber and top with a generous teaspoon of the salmon filling. Spread the filling evenly with a small spatula or press the tops down gently to spread filling to the edges. Serve immediately on a platter garnished with fresh dill and lemon slices.

Petits Choux à la Chèvre, au Miel et à la Purée de l'Ail Cuit au Four

Small Savory Cream Puffs with Goat Cheese, Honey and Roasted Garlic Purée

(YIELDS 26 TO 30 PETITES CHOUX)

Roasting whole garlic heads brings a nutty, buttery goodness and a slightly sweet flavor to the otherwise pungent bulb. Just a dab of roasted garlic atop a bed of cream-lightened fresh goat cheese seasoned with fresh thyme tastes glorious, and finishing with a drizzle of honey makes it exquisite. These bite-sized flavor nuggets make beautiful appetizers but would also round out a fresh green salad for a light, yet unforgettable meal. Like so many recipes in this book, the fillings and choux can be made ahead and stored separately. Serve at room temperature for maximum flavor.

1 Master Recipe Savory Choux Pastry (page 28)

Egg wash: 1 egg yolk, splash of water, pinch of salt, blended together

2 whole heads garlic

Drizzle of olive oil

1 cup fresh goat cheese, room temperature

2 tablespoons heavy cream

1 tablespoon finely chopped fresh thyme leaves

$1/2$ teaspoon fresh lemon juice

Sea salt or kosher salt

Freshly ground black pepper

$1/4$ cup best-quality honey, optional

Preheat oven to 425°F.

Prepare Savory Choux Pastry. Pipe onto lined baking sheets according to "Piping Size How-To" for small choux (page 19). Brush each choux lightly with egg wash and bake for 20 to 25 minutes, or until puffed and golden brown. Turn off the oven, open the door, and let the pastry stand for 5 minutes. Then remove from oven, transfer to a cooling rack, and when cool enough to handle, pierce the bottom of each choux gently with the tip of a knife. Let cool completely.

The garlic can be roasted while the choux is cooking in the same 425°F oven. Cut the papery tops off of each head, removing the top $1/4$ inch or so, or enough to expose the naked tops of the individual garlic cloves. Wrap a small sheet of aluminum foil around the bulbs, and drizzle lightly with olive oil before sealing. Bake for 45 minutes (they will take a little longer than the choux), or until softened. Remove from the oven and set aside to cool.

continued >

Meanwhile, in a small bowl, whisk together the goat cheese, cream, thyme, lemon juice, and seasonings to taste. When the garlic is cool enough to handle, squeeze the heads to release the soft, roasted flesh into a small bowl (you will end up with about $1/4$ cup), discarding the papery casings. Mash the garlic with a fork or the edge of a knife to form an instant purée. Season lightly with salt and pepper.

To assemble, gently cut through the center of each choux (horizontally) using a sharp or serrated knife, stopping just short of the other side, leaving the cap attached. Dollop about 1 tablespoon of the cheese mixture into the bottom of each choux, spreading with a knife or spatula to smooth it to the edges. Top with a smidge of the garlic purée (about $1/2$ teaspoon) and a drizzle of honey. Arrange the pastry caps neatly over the choux. Serve with fresh thyme for garnish.

Sandwiches de Petits Choux à la Salade d'Endives, Pommes et Noix au Roquefort

Small Savory Cream Puff Sandwiches of Endive, Apple, Walnut and Roquefort Salad

(YIELDS 26 TO 30 PETITES CHOUX)

The classic salad is standard and beloved fare at bistros, restaurants and in home kitchens all around France. The slight bitterness of the pale green and white endive lettuce is countered with the round, edgy richness of Roquefort and the crunch of buttery, earthy walnuts. It is also fantastique *wedged between two layers of choux. Substitute a milder blue cheese such as Bleu d'Auvergne or an American blue cheese if desired.*

1 Master Recipe Savory Choux Pastry (page 28)

Egg wash: 1 egg yolk, splash of water, pinch of salt, blended together

1/3 cup best-quality prepared mayonnaise

1/2 cup crumbled Roquefort cheese

1 tablespoon fresh lemon juice

1/2 small Granny Smith apple, cored and finely diced

Freshly ground black pepper

2 small endives, any brown ends and base trimmed, halved, cored and finely sliced

1/2 cup finely chopped walnuts

Preheat oven to 425°F.

Prepare Savory Choux Pastry. Pipe onto lined baking sheets according to "Piping Size How-To" for small choux (page 19). Brush each choux lightly with egg wash and bake for 20 to 25 minutes, or until puffed and golden brown. Turn off the oven, open the door, and let the pastry stand for 5 minutes. Then remove from oven, transfer to a cooling rack, and when cool enough to handle, pierce the bottom of each choux gently with the tip of a knife. Let cool completely.

Meanwhile, in a medium bowl, gently stir together the mayonnaise, Roquefort and lemon juice with a wooden spoon. Fold in the apple, a generous pinch of pepper, the endive and walnuts until just combined. Taste and adjust seasonings as needed.

To assemble, gently cut through the center of each choux (horizontally) using a sharp or serrated knife, stopping just short of the other side and leaving the cap attached. Place 2 teaspoons of the filling neatly in the bottom of each choux and replace the cap. Serve immediately, chilled. (*Note:* The filling can be made up to 3 hours in advance, covered tightly and refrigerated before assembling and serving.)

SANDWICHS DE CHOUX À LA SALADE DE CREVETTES
Savory Cream Puff Sandwiches of Shrimp Salad
(YIELDS 26 TO 30 PETITES CHOUX)

Have you ever noticed at cocktail parties one of the most flocked-about dishes on the buffet table is the one stacked with delicate little tea sandwiches? You can safely multiply that group by 10 if the "bread" in the sandwiches is choux puffs. This lovely, light salad of finely chopped shrimp, fresh tarragon, shallots, celery and barely-there mayonnaise is the perfect filling for savory choux puffs. It's important to chop everything very finely—practically minced—so it doesn't overwhelm the delicate choux. Roasting the shrimp until just done brings out super shrimp flavor and even a little sweetness. Make the salad a few hours ahead to allow the flavors to ripen; fill the choux just before serving. Perfect for cocktail hour, tea, bridal shower, or a light summer lunch served with a salad.

1 Master Recipe Savory Choux Pastry (page 28

Egg wash: 1 egg yolk, splash of water, pinch of salt, blended together

1 pound (16–20 count) fresh shrimp, peeled and deveined

Olive oil for drizzling

Sea salt or kosher salt

Freshly ground black pepper

3 tablespoons very finely chopped shallot

3 tablespoons very finely chopped celery

1 teaspoon finely chopped fresh tarragon leaves, plus more for garnish (optional)

2 teaspoons Champagne vinegar or white wine vinegar

1/3 cup mayonnaise

1 teaspoon Dijon mustard

Preheat oven to 425°F.

Prepare Savory Choux Pastry. Pipe onto lined baking sheets according to "Piping Size How-To" for small choux (page 19). Brush each choux lightly with egg wash and bake for 20 to 25 minutes, or until puffed and golden brown. Turn off the oven, open the door, and let the pastry stand for 5 minutes. Keep the oven turned on. Remove choux from oven, transfer to a cooling rack, and when cool enough to handle, pierce the bottom of each choux gently with the tip of a knife. Let cool completely.

Rinse the shrimp and pat dry. Toss together with the olive oil and season to taste with salt and pepper. Arrange shrimp in a single layer on one baking sheet. Roast at 425°F. until the shrimp have just turned opaque, about 7 to 8 minutes. Remove from the oven and pour out onto work surface to cool. Chop the shrimp until practically minced. Each piece of shrimp should be about the size of half a small pea. In a medium bowl, combine shrimp with remaining ingredients. Taste and adjust seasonings as needed. Cover and refrigerate for at least 3 hours before serving.

To assemble the sandwiches, cut the puffs in half horizontally, using a serrated knife. Spoon a heaping teaspoon of the salad into the bottom of each puff. Replace the top and press gently. Arrange on a platter or plate with a garnish of fresh tarragon if desired.

CROQUES MESSIEURS AUX PETITS CHOUX
Small Savory Ham and Cheese Cream Puffs

(YIELDS 26 TO 30 PETITES CHOUX)

On Parisian street corners, you're apt to find vendors selling warm-from-the-griddle crêpes filled with ham and melting Gruyère, while in bistros and brasseries it's hard to miss the ubiquitous Croque Monsieur, another kind of ham and cheese sandwich dream. So why not put the same winning flavor marriage inside a warm, savory cream puff? A little dab of a warm béchamel sauce—a simple white sauce embellished with plenty of Dijon—binds the top of the puff to the melting cheese and ham sandwich bed. Serve warm at cocktail parties or with bowls of steaming tomato soup for lunch or dinner.

1 Master Recipe Savory Choux Pastry (page 28)

Egg wash: 1 egg yolk, splash of water, pinch of salt, blended together

2 tablespoons unsalted butter

1/2 shallot or small onion (about 2 tablespoons), finely chopped

2 tablespoons all-purpose flour

1 cup skim milk

3/4 cup half & half

Sea salt or kosher salt

Freshly ground black pepper

3 tablespoons Dijon mustard

8 thick slices best-quality ham

1 1/4 cups grated Gruyère or Swiss cheese

Preheat oven to 425°F.

Prepare the Savory Choux Pastry. Pipe the warm dough onto baking sheets according to directions for small choux (page 19). Brush the choux lightly with the egg wash. Bake for 20 to 25 minutes, or until puffed and golden brown. Turn off the oven, open the door, and let the pastry stand for 5 minutes. Keep the oven turned on. Remove choux from oven, transfer to a cooling rack, and when cool enough to handle, pierce the bottom of each choux gently with the tip of a knife. Let cool completely.

In a medium saucepan, melt the butter over medium heat. When just melted, add the shallot or onion and whisk to combine. Continue whisking and cooking (without browning), until the shallot has softened, about 3 minutes. Add the flour all at once, whisking rapidly to combine. Add the milk and half & half, drizzling rapidly into the roux, whisking continually. Season to taste with salt and pepper. Continue whisking and cooking the sauce another 5 to 10 minutes, or until it has come to a gentle simmer and thickened to the consistency of thick chowder. Taste and adjust seasonings as needed. Whisk in the mustard until incorporated. Reserve warm. (*Note:* Any leftovers can be stored in the refrigerator in a sealed container for up to 3 days and gently reheated for another use.)

To assemble the sandwich puffs, stack the ham in two piles of 4 slices each. Using a small round biscuit cutter, shot glass, or anything round and about the size of the choux, cut through the stack to yield about 32 rounds of ham (you should be able to get 16 rounds from each stack). Using a serrated knife, slice horizontally through the choux puffs; arrange the tops on the work surface so you know which bottoms and tops go together. Top each bottom half with a slice of ham and about 1 teaspoon of the grated cheese. Arrange the puff bottoms on a baking sheet in a single layer under a hot broiler. Broil for 2 minutes, or until the cheese is melted and bubbling. Remove from oven and top each with a generous dollop of the warm sauce and its corresponding choux top. Serve immediately. These are best warm but are also fine at room temperature. Any leftover sauce can be used to lightly garnish the platter or individual plates.

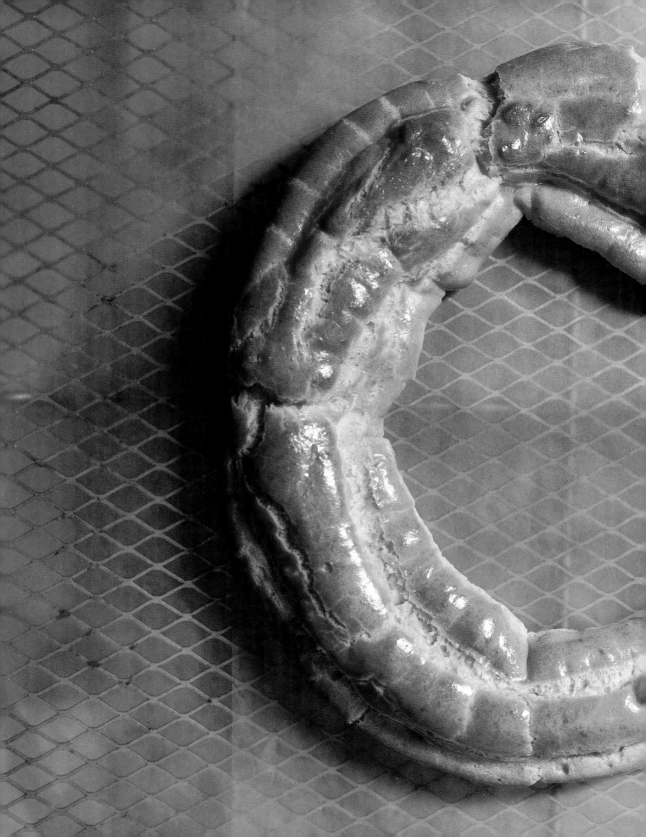

CHAPTER 2

LES ÉCLAIRS SAVOUREUX
Savory Éclairs and Choux Rings

Baby éclairs make the perfect wrap for elegant little plays on bacon, avocado and tomato sandwiches and Caesar salads, while choux rings small and large dress up silky chicken liver pâté and a fresh twist on Provençale Salade Niçoise in this chapter.

The delicious fillings and choux casings in each of these tempting dishes can be prepared ahead separately and assembled at the last minute, making for original, fun and delicious food whenever a celebration is called for.

Petits Éclairs à la Mousse d'Avocat au Bacon et aux Tomates

Small Éclairs with Avocado Mousse, Bacon and Tomatoes

(YIELDS 22 TO 26 PETITS ÉCLAIRS)

Verdant as a garden with a bright green avocado mousse, layers of finely sliced tomatoes, and shards of crunchy, salty bacon, this little bundle is packed with soul-satisfying flavor and texture in every bite. Think of it as an elegant interpretation of a good, old-fashioned American BLT.

1 Master Recipe Savory Choux Pastry (page 28)
Egg wash: 1 egg yolk, splash of water, pinch of salt, blended together

For the avocado mousse:
1 ripe avocado, halved, pitted and skin removed
1 tablespoon fresh lemon juice
1 tablespoon olive oil

1 teaspoon heavy cream (do not substitute a lesser fat cream or it may curdle)
Sea salt or kosher salt
Freshly ground black pepper
2 tablespoons very finely chopped shallots
2 tablespoons finely chopped chives, plus more for garnish
8 slices bacon
14 grape tomatoes, rinsed and thinly sliced

Preheat oven to 425°F.

Prepare Savory Choux Pastry. Pipe onto lined baking sheets according to directions for small éclairs (page 19). Brush each choux lightly with egg wash and bake for 20 to 25 minutes, or until puffed and golden brown. Turn off the oven, open the door, and let the pastry stand for 5 minutes. Remove choux from oven, transfer to a cooling rack, and when cool enough to handle, pierce the bottom of each choux gently with the tip of a knife. Let cool completely.

In a medium bowl, combine the avocado, lemon juice, olive oil and cream, and mash with the tines of a fork or a potato masher until smooth and fluffy; alternatively, purée in a food processor. Season to taste with salt and pepper. Fold in the shallots and chives and combine until smooth. Set aside. (*Note:* The mousse can be prepared a few hours in advance, covered tightly and refrigerated.)

Meanwhile, heat a large sauté pan over medium-high heat. Arrange the bacon in a single layer and cook on each side until well browned, about 3 minutes. Remove from the pan and drain on paper towels. Cut the bacon into 3-inch lengths and set aside.

To assemble, slice the éclairs in half horizontally, cutting all the way through. Reserve the tops and bottoms alongside their matching half. With a small spatula, spread 1 heaping tablespoon of the avocado mousse neatly on the bottom of each éclair. Top with a trimmed piece of bacon and 3 slices of tomato, arranged nicely along the length of the éclair. Serve immediately, garnished with fresh chives.

PETITS ÉCLAIRS À LA SALADE DE CAESAR AU BEURRE D'ANCHOIS

Small Éclairs Caesar Salad-Style with Anchovy Butter

(YIELDS 22 TO 26 PETITS ÉCLAIRS)

Rife with the pungent fresh flavors of anchovies, garlic and lemon, these éclairs play an ode to the classic Caesar salad and are finished with the buttery crunch of finely sliced Romaine lettuce. Toss any remaining butter with warm pasta for a follow-up feast to these crowd-pleasing and beautiful éclair treats.

1 Master Recipe Savory Choux Pastry (page 28)
Egg wash: 1 egg yolk, splash of water, pinch of salt, blended together

For the anchovy butter:

1 cup (2 sticks) unsalted butter, room temperature
1/4 cup (one 3.5 ounce jar) anchovies, drained and smashed into a purée with the edge of a chef's knife
1/4 cup finely chopped fresh parsley leaves

2 large cloves garlic, peeled, and smashed into a purée with the edge of a chef's knife
Juice of 1/2 lemon
Pinch of sea salt or kosher salt
Freshly ground black pepper

12 leaves Romaine lettuce for garnish, brown spots removed, washed, dried, stacked and cut into a fine dice

Preheat oven to 425°F.

Prepare Savory Choux Pastry. Pipe onto lined baking sheets according to "Piping Size How-To" for small éclairs (page 19). Brush each choux lightly with egg wash and bake for 20 to 25 minutes, or until puffed and golden brown. Turn off the oven, open the door, and let the pastry stand for 5 minutes. Remove choux from oven, transfer to a cooling rack, and when cool enough to handle, pierce the bottom of each éclair gently with the tip of a knife. Let cool completely.

In a medium bowl, combine the butter, anchovies, parsley, garlic, and lemon. Blend with a wooden spoon to combine. Season to taste with salt and a generous dash of pepper. (*Note:* The butter will develop deeper flavors if made an hour ahead of assembling the éclairs. If desired, refrigerate overnight and bring to room temperature before assembling.)

To assemble, slice the éclairs in half horizontally, cutting all the way through. Reserve the tops and bottoms alongside their matching half. With a small spatula, spread 1 heaping tablespoon of the anchovy butter on the bottom of each éclair. Top with a neatly arranged layer of the sliced Romaine, about 1 tablespoon per éclair. Replace top half, and serve immediately, garnished with fresh parsley.

SALADE NIÇOISE COMPOSÉE DANS UND GROS ROND DE PÂTE À CHOUX
Composed Niçois Salad in a Large Savory Choux Ring

(YIELDS 12 TO 14 APPETIZER PORTIONS)

This composed Salade Niçoise will take center stage at your next celebration. As well suited to a Super Bowl party as a wedding shower, the salad is piled up inside the ring and arranged beautifully on a platter. Cut into 2-inch lengths just before serving. Think of it as a gorgeous, grown-up tuna sandwich with a Provençale twist.

1 Master Recipe Savory Choux Pastry (page 28)

Egg wash: 1 egg yolk, splash of water, pinch of salt, blended together

For the filling:

2 (5-ounce) cans albacore tuna in water, drained

1/2 small onion, very finely chopped

1/2 small stalk celery, very finely chopped

2 sardines, smashed and finely chopped

15 pitted kalamata olives, finely chopped

1 tablespoon finely chopped fresh parsley leaves

1 tablespoon red wine vinegar

1 tablespoon Dijon mustard

1/4 cup plus 1 teaspoon mayonnaise

Freshly ground black pepper

Garnishes:

1/4 cup drained pimentos

2 Roma tomatoes, very thinly sliced

3 leaves Romaine lettuce cut into 1-inch squares

Preheat oven to 425°F. Prepare Savory Choux Pastry. Pipe onto lined baking sheets according to "Piping Size How-To" for large rings (page 19). Brush lightly with egg wash and bake for 20 to 22 minutes, or until puffed and golden brown. Reduce heat to 375°F and bake 10 to 15 minutes more, until well set in the center. Turn off the oven, open the door, and let the pastry stand for 5 minutes. Then remove from oven and transfer to a pastry rack to cool. When cool enough to handle, pierce the bottom of the ring in 4 or 5 spots with the tip of a knife, and cool completely.

In a medium bowl, combine the tuna, onion, celery, sardines, olives, parsley, vinegar, mustard and mayonnaise. Stir to combine. Season to taste with pepper. (No salt needed, since the anchovies are salty.)

Just before serving, carefully slice the ring in half horizontally, as evenly as possible, with a sharp serrated knife. Using a spatula, neatly arrange the filling on the bottom of the choux ring. Arrange an even layer of the pimentos, topped with a layer of tomatoes, and finishing with a light layer of lettuce. Place the choux top on the salad. Cut just before serving.

Pâté de Foies de Volailles aux Pruneaux sur les Petits Ronds de Pâte à Choux

Chicken Liver Pâté with Prunes on Small Savory Choux Rings

(6 TO 12 INDIVIDUAL SERVINGS; SEE BELOW)

Cognac-macerated prunes and the flavor of thyme threaded ever so faintly throughout give this luscious, smooth, decadent pâté sweet notes of the Alsace region of France. The pâté makes enough for at least 12 rings, so two batches of choux will be needed to use up all the pâté. Alternatively, make one batch of choux and use the leftover pâté in other ways. Pâté lovers will not be able to escape its grasp, however, and it will be gone before you know it. The rings look beautiful with a nice layer of the pâté in the center. Assemble just before serving.

2 batches Master Recipe Savory Choux Pastry
   (page 28)
Egg wash: 1 egg yolk, splash of water, pinch of salt,
   blended together

For the pâté:
1 cup pitted prunes
4 tablespoons best-quality cognac
1 pound drained chicken livers, patted dry
1 large shallot, peeled and very thinly sliced

3 cloves garlic, peeled and smashed
1 bay leaf
1 cup water
1 teaspoon sea salt or kosher salt, plus more
1 3/4 stick unsalted butter, room temperature
Reserved cognac from the prunes, plus 1 tablespoon
   additional cognac
1 tablespoon finely chopped fresh thyme leaves
Freshly ground black pepper

Preheat oven to 425°F.

Prepare Savory Choux Pastry. Pipe onto lined baking sheets according to "Piping Size How-To" for small rings (page 19). Brush lightly with egg wash and bake for 25 minutes, or until puffed and golden brown. Turn off the oven, open the door, and let the pastry stand for 5 minutes. Remove choux from oven, transfer to a cooling rack, and when cool enough to handle, pierce the bottom of each ring gently in two or three spots with the tip of a knife. Let cool completely.

Meanwhile, prepare the pâté. Combine the prunes and cognac in a small glass bowl. Heat in the microwave on high for 1 minute. Alternatively, bring to a simmer in a small saucepan on the stovetop over medium-high heat and cook for 3 minutes. Set aside.

In a large saucepan, combine the chicken livers, shallot, garlic, bay leaf, water and 1 teaspoon salt. Bring to a simmer over medium-high heat then reduce to low. Cook gently, spooning water over the liver as needed to poach. Cook for about 5 to 7 minutes, or until the livers are tender with a pale pink center. Remove from the heat and let them sit for 5 minutes.

Remove the bay leaf. Remove the solids from the liquid with a slotted spoon and place into the bowl of a food processor fitted with a metal blade. Purée for about 30 seconds to blend. Press the cognac out of the reserved prunes into the bowl of the food processor and pulse 5 to 10 times to combine. Turn the purée out into a medium bowl. Chop the prunes finely and fold into the purée with the additional tablespoon of Cognac and fresh thyme. Taste and adjust seasonings. Cover tightly with plastic wrap pressed down to the top of the pâté to avoid oxidation, and refrigerate at least 3 to 4 hours and up to 24 hours to set.

To serve, cut the rings in half horizontally with a sharp serrated knife. Using a spatula, spread about $^1/_2$ inch of the pâté on the bottom of each ring. Top with their respective choux tops. Plate individually and garnish with fresh thyme and a few prunes. Best served at room temperature for maximum flavor.

CHAPTER 3

LES CHOUX À LA CRÈME SUCRÉES ET LES CHANGEMENTS
Sweet Cream Puffs, Choux Rings, and Variations

Just like their savory partners in taste-tempting crime, sweet cream puffs can be filled with almost any sweet flavor pairing imaginable, as long as the flavors are compatible. Flavored whipped cream, pastry cream, butter cream, ganache and more are the stuff of cream puff dreams. Hot takes in the form of beignets and cold takes in the form of ice cream-filled profiteroles also take center stage.

The process of preparing sweet choux pastry is exactly the same as preparing savory choux pastry, with two small differences: the addition of a small amount of sugar (1 tablespoon) and reducing the amount of salt from $1/2$ teaspoon to $1/4$ teaspoon. All else remains the same. The end result is, naturally, vaguely sweeter than savory choux and just a note less salty. It's the perfect contrast for all of the wonderful sweet creams, fillings, ice creams and sauces with which a sweet cream puff can be served.

Recette Maîtresse pour la Pâte à Choux Sucrée
Master Recipe for Sweet Choux Pastry
(for preparing sweet choux puffs, éclairs and rings)

(YIELDS 24 TO 30 PETITS CHOUX, 12 TO 16 GROS CHOUX, 22 TO 26 PETITS ÉCLAIRS, 12 TO 16 GROS ÉCLAIRS)

For a detailed description of the choux pastry preparation process, see "De-mystifying the Puff" (page 15) and "Making Choux the Right Way" (page 16). This recipe provides the ingredient quantities and a more abbreviated description.

1 cup water

3/4 stick (3 ounces) unsalted butter, cold, cut into
   1/2-inch cubes

1/2 cup bread flour

1/2 cup all-purpose flour

1 tablespoon sugar

1/4 teaspoon sea salt or kosher salt

4 large eggs (about 1 cup), room temperature,
   beaten together

Egg wash: 1 egg yolk, splash of water, pinch of salt,
   blended together

Preheat the oven according to specific recipe instructions that follow in this book (temperatures will vary according to choux size). Line two half-sheet baking pans with silicon mats or parchment paper. Measure all the ingredients and have them ready before starting to prepare the dough.

In a medium, heavy-bottom saucepan, heat the water and butter together over medium-high heat, stirring once or twice to help the butter melt. Once melted, reduce heat to medium.

Sift together the two flours and salt over a medium bowl. Add the sifted dry ingredients all at once to the water mixture, and set the bowl nearby. Stir the dough vigorously with a wooden spoon to bring it together. Continue stirring, less vigorously, until the pastry pulls away from the sides of the pan and forms a uniform ball. Turn the pastry out into the reserved bowl and let sit for about 1 minute, or until the pastry is cool enough to touch comfortably with your fingertip for at least 10 seconds. Add half of the beaten eggs (about 1/2 cup) to the pastry. Stir vigorously until the pastry looks uniform and glossy, about 1 minute. Add half of the remaining egg mixture (about 1/4 cup) and continue to stir until the pastry is uniform and glossy, about 1 minute. Repeat with the remaining egg mixture.

While the pastry is still warm, pipe and bake the pastry according to specific recipe directions. (For a more detailed overview, see "Piping and Scooping" page 18 and "Piping Size How-To," page 19). Brush the top of each pastry with a light coating of egg wash, being careful not to let the wash drip down the sides of the pastry.

CHOUX À LA CRÈME DE NOIX DE COCO
Coconut Cream Puffs

(YIELDS 24 TO 30 PETITS CHOUX, OR 12 TO 14 GROS CHOUX)

Whipped cream folded into the pastry cream gives this variation a light-as-air texture. Toasted coconut is also folded in, and the whole thing is topped with chocolate and more coconut for garnish. The end result is coconut crazy good! The whipped cream makes the pastry cream a little bit less stable, so y to serve the cream puffs within 1 to 2 hours after filling.

1 Master Recipe Sweet Choux Pastry (page 62)
$^1/_2$ Master Recipe Pastry Cream (page 66)
$^1/_4$ cup plus 3 tablespoons dried coconut flakes

$^1/_2$ cup cold whipping cream
$^1/_2$ recipe Ganache/Hot Chocolate Sauce
  (page 113)

Preheat oven to 425°F. Prepare Sweet Choux Pastry. Pipe small or large choux (see page 19) onto lined baking sheets. Brush lightly with egg wash and bake for 20 to 25 minutes for small and 30 to 35 minutes for large, or until puffed and golden brown. Turn off the oven, open the door, and let the pastry stand for 5 minutes. Remove choux from oven, transfer to a cooling rack, pierce the bottom of each gently with the tip of a knife.

Prepare the Pastry Cream and chill in the refrigerator for 2 to 3 hours.

Combine all the coconut flakes in a small sauté pan and toast over medium-high heat, tossing occasionally, until lightly tanned and fragrant, about 2 minutes. Set aside.

In a chilled medium-size stainless steel, copper or glass bowl, mount the whipped cream until firm points form. If using a whisk, work quickly, lifting under the cream to aerate and mount. It can also be mounted using a hand-held blender. Either way, it will take about 3 minutes to get there. To incorporate into the pastry cream, whisk half of the whipped cream into the pastry cream. Fold in the remainder, blending carefully with a wooden spoon until the cream is just incorporated but not beaten up. It should be light and airy. Gently fold in $^1/_4$ cup toasted coconut flakes (reserving 3 tablespoons for garnish). Chill for at least 1 hour before filling the choux.

To fill the choux, pipe the pastry cream mixture in through the bottom of the choux— 1 teaspoon for petits choux or 1 tablespoon for gros choux—using a #802 pastry tip.

Prepare the Ganache and cool at room temperature for 1 hour before garnishing so that it has had time to set up to "drizzle" stage. Drizzle 1 teaspoon over petits choux and 1 tablespoon over gros choux. Sprinkle $^1/_4$ teaspoon of the reserved 3 tablespoons toasted coconut flakes over the center of each cream puff. Chill for up to 2 hours before serving.

Suggested sauce pairing: Crème Anglaise (page 114) or Raspberry Sauce (page 117).

Choux à la Crème de Potiron et Canelle aux Pacanes

Cinnamon-Spiced Pumpkin Pecan Cream Puffs

(YIELDS 24 TO 30 PETITS CHOUX)

Delicate notes of cinnamon folded into creamed mascarpone and cream cheese, combined with the soft color and flavor glow of pumpkin purée folded into the choux, recall the deliciousness of fresh pumpkin pie topped with whipped cream. The choux can be filled several hours ahead and chilled before serving. Bring to room temperature before plating. (Note: Mascarpone is an Italian sweet cream cheese usually found in the gourmet cheese section of most grocery stores. If unavailable, substitute cream cheese.)

1 Master Recipe Sweet Choux Pastry (page 62)
1/4 cup plus 1 tablespoon canned pumpkin purée
Egg wash: 1 egg yolk, splash of water, pinch of salt
   blended together

For the filling:
1 cup mascarpone cheese, room temperature
1/2 cup cream cheese, room temperature
1/4 cup powdered sugar
1 teaspoon vanilla extract

1/2 teaspoon ground nutmeg
1/2 teaspoon ground ginger
1 teaspoon cognac
3 tablespoons whipping cream
Pinch of sea salt or kosher salt
1/4 cup finely chopped pecans

For garnishing:
1/4 cup powdered sugar
1 teaspoon ground cinnamon

Preheat oven to 425°F. Prepare Sweet Choux Pastry, whisking the pumpkin purée into the water and butter mixture to incorporate. Proceed with the pastry as otherwise directed. Pipe onto lined baking sheets according to "Piping Size How-To" for small choux (page 19). Brush each choux lightly with egg wash and bake for 20 to 25 minutes, or until puffed and golden brown. Turn off the oven, open the door, and let the pastry stand for 5 minutes. Remove choux to a cooling rack, and pierce the bottom of each gently with the tip of a knife. Let cool completely.

To prepare the filling, combine all of the ingredients, except the pecans, in a small bowl, blending well with a whisk until smooth. Fold in the pecans with a wooden spoon to combine. Cut the cooled, baked choux in half vertically with a serrated knife. To fill, either spread about 1 teaspoon of the filling into each with a small spatula or pipe in a small circular motion using a #863 star tip onto the bottom of each choux. Return the caps to their respective choux. Combine powdered sugar with cinnamon and garnish by sifting lightly over the top of each choux.

Suggested sauce pairing: These puffs are beautiful plain but would also be lovely seated in a pool of cool Crème Anglaise (page 114).

RECETTE MAÎTRESSE POUR LA CRÈME PÂTISSIÈRE
Master Recipe for Pastry Cream

(YIELDS 2¹/₂ CUPS)

This cornerstone custard filling for both cream puffs and éclairs is mildly sweet, unctuous and pale gold in color. Egg yolks and cornstarch work together to thicken the custard, while whole milk lends creamy flavor. The custard can be made even richer by substituting half & half or cream, if desired. There is nothing difficult about preparing pastry cream, but it deserves your full attention and a ready whisking arm. The custard needs to be pulled away from the warm edges and bottom of the pan to prevent the eggs from scrambling into a sweet mess. If that starts to happen, pull the pan off the heat immediately, whisk rapidly, and strain through a china cap. Even with a non-curdled custard, straining is an important step to eliminate any stray egg solids. After the custard is cooled, it holds nicely for up to 3 days in the refrigerator.

Because this is such a sturdy cream with a mild flavor, it lends itself to myriad variations: whip in chopped chocolate while the cream is warm, or fold coffee, coconut, citrus, fresh fruit and berry coulis, nuts or practically anything you can think of into the cold custard before piping into the cream puffs and éclairs. And, yes, this is a piping situation. The cream is tender in texture and doesn't hold its shape super well. For this reason, it is best presented piped into the interior of a puff or an éclair, instead of piped into the center of halved pastries.

A close cousin to Crème Anglaise (page 114), this will become a staple in your sweet choux kitchen. This master recipe yields enough pastry cream to fill 1 Master Recipe Sweet Choux Pastry of any size, shape or form.

2 cups warm milk	3 tablespoons cornstarch
6 egg yolks	1 tablespoon unsalted butter
¹/₂ cup sugar	1 tablespoon vanilla extract
Generous pinch of sea salt or kosher salt	

Heat the milk in a medium saucepan over medium heat until it reaches a very low simmer, about 3 minutes.

In a medium bowl, whisk the eggs together vigorously until they are lemony in color and thickened, about 2 minutes. Sift together the sugar, salt and cornstarch and add all at once to the eggs. Whisk vigorously for another minute. The mixture will have a glossy sheen. Very gradually at first, drizzle the warm milk into the egg mixture, whisking all the while. Add the remaining milk in thirds, whisking constantly. Strain the mixture through a China cap and return the pastry cream

continued >

to the same pan used to heat the milk. Whisk vigorously over medium-low heat. The cream will start to thicken almost instantly. Continue cooking for 1 to 2 minutes, or until the cream is thick enough to hold in a spoon, like a custard or pudding. Using a spatula, guide the custard into a clean glass bowl. Whisk in the butter and vanilla extract until combined. Cover with plastic wrap, pressing it down over the top of the cream to prevent a skin from forming. Refrigerate until chilled and set.

CHOUQUETTES
Sugar-Crusted Cream Puffs

(YIELDS 26 TO 30 PETITS CHOUX)

These precious little sweet treats are as simple as can be and commonly available at the counters of French patisseries, usually warm from the oven in little paper bags. A favorite after-school snack for French children, chouquettes *are prepared by piping (or plopping) small choux, brushing them with egg wash, and coating the sides and tops with crunchy, large-crystal sugar (like we used to garnish the Creamsicle Cream Puffs, page 76). Feel free to mix up the colors and textures for added fun.*

1 Master Recipe Sweet Choux Pastry (page 62)
Egg wash: 1 egg yolk, splash of water, pinch of salt,
   blended together

1¼ cups colored sugar crystals

Preheat oven to 425°F.

Prepare the Sweet Choux Pastry according to directions. Pipe the warm dough onto lined baking sheets according to directions for small choux (page 19). Brush the choux lightly with the egg wash. Drizzle the top and sides of each with about 1 teaspoon sugar crystals and press the crystals gently into the choux using the tips of your fingers. Bake for 20 to 25 minutes, or until puffed and golden brown. Turn off the oven, open the door, and let the pastry stand for 5 minutes. Remove choux from the oven, transfer to a cooling rack, and when cool enough to handle, pierce the bottom of each choux gently with the tip of a knife. Let cool completely.

Serve warm or at room temperature. Like regular choux, they freeze well. Simply thaw and reheat in a 375°F oven for a few minutes to crisp before serving.

CHOUX À LA CRÈME PÂTISSIÈRE SANGUINE AVEC GANACHE ET SEL D'ERABLE

Cream Puffs with Blood Orange Pastry Cream, Chocolate Cream and Maple Salt

(YIELDS 24 TO 30 PETITS CHOUX, OR 12 TO 14 GROS CHOUX)

Blood oranges are exquisite fruits, found during winter months at most grocery stores. Another fresh sweet orange juice, such as tangerine or navel, can be substituted. In this recipe, the juice is reduced to a glaze and folded into the pastry cream, giving it exotic color and flavor. The puffs are topped with a semi-firm ganache, which works magic with the delicate orange flavor of the pastry cream. A pinch of seasoned maple salt (available at most specialty spice shops) on top of each adds a pleasant savory/salty finish and a delightful crunch. If you can't find maple salt, simply substitute coarse sea salt or kosher salt.

$^1/_2$ cup fresh blood orange juice

1 Master Recipe Sweet Choux Pastry (page 62)

1 Master Recipe Pastry Cream (page 66)

Zest of 2 blood oranges, finely chopped

$^1/_4$ teaspoon orange extract

$^1/_2$ recipe Ganache/Hot Chocolate Sauce (page 113)

1 teaspoon coarse maple salt to garnish

Reduce blood orange juice down to 1 tablespoon in a small saucepan over medium-high heat. Let cool to room temperature.

Preheat oven to 425°F. Prepare Sweet Choux Pastry. Pipe onto lined baking sheets, either small or large choux (page 19). Brush lightly with egg wash and bake for 20 to 25 minutes for small and 30 to 35 minutes for large, or until puffed and golden brown. Turn off the oven, open the door, and let the pastry stand for 5 minutes. Remove choux to a cooling rack, and pierce the bottom of each gently with the tip of a knife.

Prepare the Pastry Cream, stirring in the zest and cooled reduced juice after the pastry cream is strained—at the same time as the orange extract. Chill for at least 1 hour.

To fill the choux, pipe 1 teaspoon of pastry cream for petits choux or 1 tablespoon of pastry cream for gros choux, using a #802 pastry tip.

Prepare the Ganache and cool at room temperature for 1 hour before garnishing so it has had time to set up to "drizzle" stage. Drizzle 1 teaspoon over petits choux and 1 tablespoon over gros choux. Sprinkle a pinch of maple salt in the center of each cream puff. Chill for up to 3 hours before serving.

Suggested sauce pairings: Crème Anglaise (page 114) or Sweetened Vanilla Cream Sauce (page 112). Alternatively, make a full recipe of the ganache and heat gently over low heat to serve as a warm sauce.

CHOUX À LA CRÈME PÂTISSIÈRE DES AMANDES, NOIX DE COCO ET DE CHOCOLAT
Almond Joy Cream Puffs

(YIELDS 24 TO 30 PETITS CHOUX, OR 12 TO 14 GROS CHOUX)

A cool coconut pastry cream filling with a chocolate glaze brings to mind the revered American candy bar, with a decidedly French twist. This filling works beautifully for either small or large choux, but the filling needs to be piped in through the bottom of each whole, uncut puff. Spoon some cooled chocolate sauce over the top of each and drizzle with a smattering of almonds, and you are on your way to cream puff nirvana.

1 Master Recipe Sweet Choux Pastry (page 62)

1 Master Recipe Pastry Cream (page 66)

1 cup dried coconut flakes

$^1\!/_2$ recipe Ganache/Hot Chocolate Sauce (page 113)

$^1\!/_2$ cup finely chopped salted almonds to garnish

Preheat oven to 425°F.

Prepare Sweet Choux Pastry. Pipe onto lined baking sheets according to "Piping Size How-To" for small choux or large choux (page 19). Brush each choux lightly with egg wash and bake for 20 to 25 minutes for small and 30 to 35 minutes for large, or until puffed and golden brown. Turn off the oven, open the door, and let the pastry stand for 5 minutes. Remove choux to a cooling rack, and pierce the bottom of each gently with the tip of a knife. Let cool completely.

Prepare the Pastry Cream, stirring in the coconut after the pastry cream is strained, adding it at the same time as the vanilla. Stir to incorporate. Chill for at least 1 hour before filling the choux.

To fill the choux, pipe 1 teaspoon of pastry cream for small choux or 1 tablespoon of pastry cream for large choux through the bottom of the pastry, using a #802 pastry tip.

Prepare the Hot Chocolate Sauce and cool at room temperature for 1 hour before garnishing so it has had time to set up to "drizzle" stage. Drizzle 1 teaspoon over small choux and 1 table-spoon over large choux. Sprinkle chopped almonds over each choux to finish. Chill for up to 3 hours before serving.

Suggested sauce pairings: Crème Anglaise (page 114) or Sweetened Vanilla Cream Sauce (page 112). Alternatively, make a full recipe of the Hot chocolate Sauce and heat gently over low heat to serve as a warm sauce.

GROS CHOUX À LA CRÈME
PÂTISSIÈRE DE NUTELLA ET CAFÉ
Large Cream Puffs with Nutella and Coffee
Pastry Cream

(YIELDS 16 GROS CHOUX)

I discovered Nutella for the first time in a crêpe from a corner vendor in Paris many moons ago. It was love at first bite. Now readily available in the States, the creamy hazelnut cream, kissed with a faint amount of chocolate, is luscious whisked into pastry cream. A splash of hazelnut and coffee liqueurs blended in further perfumes the rich, firm cream with this classic flavor pairing. Because the filling has a rich color and firm texture, I like to be able to see it. So I recommend simply placing a dollop in the center of each puff, spreading lightly and replacing the cap. A light glaze of coffee and Nutella royal icing goes on top.

1 Master Recipe Sweet Choux Pastry (page 62)

1/2 cup of Master Recipe Pastry Cream (page 66)

1/2 cup Nutella

Generous pinch of sea salt or kosher salt

1 teaspoon hazelnut liqueur

1 teaspoon coffee liqueur

For the royal icing:

1/2 cup powdered sugar

1 tablespoon plus 1 teaspoon strong coffee

1 teaspoon Nutella

Generous pinch of sea salt or kosher salt

Preheat oven to 425°F. Prepare Sweet Choux Pastry. Pipe onto lined baking sheets according to sizing for large choux (page 19). Brush each choux lightly with egg wash and bake for 30 to 35 minutes, or until golden brown. Turn off the oven, open the door, and let the pastry stand for 5 minutes. Remove choux to a cooling rack, and pierce the bottom of each gently with the tip of a knife.

Prepare the Pastry Cream and refrigerate for 2 to 3 hours. To prepare the filling, whisk together the pastry cream, Nutella, salt, and liqueurs in a medium bowl until smooth.

To prepare the royal icing, in a separate small bowl, whisk together the powdered sugar, coffee, Nutella and salt.

Slice each choux in half, horizontally, using a serrated knife. "Plop" a generous 1 to 2 tablespoons of the filling onto the bottom of each. Spread gently with a spatula to the edges, and top each with its choux lid. Using the back of a teaspoon or a fingertip, glaze the top of each lightly with royal icing. Chill for up to 3 hours before serving.

Suggested sauce pairings: Crème Anglaise (page 114), Sweetened Vanilla Cream Sauce (page 112) or Raspberry Sauce (page 117). (*Note:* If using the raspberry sauce, omit the ganache glaze and substitute a light dusting of powdered sugar on top of each choux.)

Choux à la Crème Pâtissière de Banane, Rhum, Cassonade et Beurre
Bananas Foster Cream Puffs

(YIELDS 24 TO 30 PETITS CHOUX)

Although the classic dessert was created at Brennan's in New Orleans, the flavors of butter, cinnamon and bourbon (or substitute dark rum) are universally loved. In this recipe, ripe bananas are sautéed in butter until they soften and are seasoned with all of the above and then some. The cooled mixture is then puréed and stirred into whipped, room-temperature butter, rendering a basic form of a classic butter cream. A larger pastry tip to fill the choux ensures any banana chunks will flow freely into the puffs. The bananas hidden inside the puffs pop with a cinnamon spice surprise in each bite. Be careful to whip the butter at room temperature or it will clump, and add the banana mixture to the butter only after it has cooled, or it will melt. Des enfants love these!

1 Master Recipe Sweet Choux Pastry (page 62)

For the filling:
2 tablespoons unsalted butter
2 firm ripe bananas, peeled and cut into
  $1/2$-inch dice
$1/2$ cup dark brown sugar
$1/2$ teaspoon sea salt or kosher salt
1 teaspoon ground cinnamon
1 tablespoon bourbon (or rum)
1 teaspoon vanilla extract

$3/4$ cup ($1^1/2$ sticks) unsalted butter, room
  temperature
2 tablespoons heavy cream

For the royal icing:
$1/2$ cup powdered sugar
2 teaspoons bourbon
1 teaspoon heavy cream
Pinch of sea salt or kosher salt
$1/4$ teaspoon ground cinnamon

Preheat oven to 425°F.

Prepare Sweet Choux Pastry. Pipe onto lined baking sheets according to "Piping Size How-To" for small choux (page 19). Brush each choux lightly with egg wash and bake for 20 to 25 minutes, or until puffed and golden brown. Turn off the oven, open the door, and let the pastry stand for 5 minutes. Remove choux to a cooling rack, and pierce the bottom of each gently with the tip of a knife. Let cool completely.

To prepare the filling, in a large sauté pan, melt the butter over medium heat. Add the bananas, increase heat to medium-high, and cook for 3 minutes, or until the bananas begin to soften. Add the remaining filling ingredients. Swirl the pan to combine. Cook another 2 or 3 minutes, until the liquids have reduced to a glaze on the bottom of the pan. Turn out into a small bowl and refrigerate to chill.

Meanwhile, whip the butter with a blender on medium speed in a medium bowl until it is light and frothy, about 2 minutes. When the banana mixture is cold, beat it into the whipped butter on medium speed until thoroughly incorporated, about 1 minute. Spoon the filling into a pastry bag fitted with a #806 round tip. Pipe a generous teaspoon into each choux, or until it just begins to swell with the filling.

Combine the royal icing ingredients in a small bowl and whisk until smooth. Using a fingertip or the back of a teaspoon, glaze each choux with a scant amount of icing, about $1/2$ teaspoon. Refrigerate for up to 3 hours before serving.

Suggested sauce pairings: Crème Anglaise (page 114), Sweetened Vanilla Cream Sauce (page 112), or Caramel Sauce (page 118).

CHOUX À LA CRÈME D'ORANGE ET VANILLE
Creamsicle Cream Puffs
(YIELDS 24 TO 30 PETITS CHOUX, OR 12 TO 14 GROS CHOUX)

Ooh la la! These are indeed dreamy treats. Whipped cream lightly infused with bright orange flavoring is a dead ringer for an orange Creamsicle pop. Served cold on a bed of hot chocolate sauce, these treats move the soul into the next dimension—they are that delicious and delightfully easy to prepare. The lightly tinged orange filling is so pretty, it's best to just plop it into the center of the choux so everyone can see it. These are best served lightly frozen, contrasting with the hot sauce. If you freeze them overnight or longer, be sure to take them out of the freezer 30 minutes before serving. Orange-tinted granulated sugar makes a tres jolie finish on top of the royal icing.

1 Master Recipe Sweet Choux Pastry (page 62)

For the filling:
3 tablespoons fresh orange juice (don't substitute concentrate)

1 cup cold whipping cream

Zest of 1 orange, finely chopped (about 1 teaspoon)

$1/4$ teaspoon orange extract

$1/2$ teaspoon vanilla extract

$1/4$ cup powdered sugar

Reserved reduced orange juice

For the royal icing:
$1/4$ cup powdered sugar

$1/4$ teaspoon orange extract

2 tablespoons heavy cream

Orange-colored granulated sugar

Preheat oven to 425°F. Prepare Sweet Choux Pastry. Pipe onto lined baking sheets according to "Piping Size How-To" for small choux or large choux (page 19). Brush each choux lightly with egg wash and bake for 20 to 25 minutes for small and 30 to 35 minutes for large, or until puffed and golden brown. Turn off the oven, open the door, and let the pastry stand for 5 minutes. Remove choux to a cooling rack; when cool enough to handle, pierce the bottom of each gently with the tip of a knife. Let cool completely.

To prepare the filling, in a small saucepan, reduce the orange juice to 1 teaspoon over high heat, 1 to 2 minutes. Turn out into a small bowl and refrigerate to cool. In a large, cold bowl, combine the remaining filling ingredients, including the cooled teaspoon of orange juice. Using a blender, blend on medium speed until the cream is whipped to firm peaks.

Prepare the royal icing by stirring together the ingredients in a small bowl until smooth and incorporated. To fill the choux, cut each in half horizontally. Plop a heaping teaspoon (for small) or a heaping 1 1/2 tablespoons (for large) in the center of each choux. Replace the respective caps, trying not to press down too firmly on the whipped cream. Glaze each lightly with the royal icing, using a fingertip or the back of a teaspoon. Top with a pinch of the orange sugar (from the baking aisle, or color your own). Freeze for at least 30 minutes before serving to set the cream.

Suggested sauce pairing: These were made to be served with Hot Chocolate Sauce (page 113). Almost no other sauce will compare, as orange and chocolate work so well together.

CHOUX À LA CRÈME AU BEURRE AU CAFÉ, GLAÇAGE AU CARAMEL

Cream Puffs with Coffee Buttercream and a Caramel Glaze

(YIELDS 24 TO 30 PETITS CHOUX)

A fluffy, silky-smooth buttercream flavored with coffee extract and coffee liqueur fills the center of these cream puffs, which are topped with a bit of rich caramel glaze. These can be assembled and chilled several hours before serving. Because the buttercream is so tender, it's best to pipe it into the center of each choux.

1 Recipe Caramel Sauce (page 118)
1 Master Recipe Sweet Choux Pastry (page 62)

For the buttercream filling:
2 sticks (1 cup) unsalted butter, room temperature
1/2 cup powdered sugar

Pinch of sea salt or kosher salt
1/3 cup cream cheese, room temperature
3 teaspoons coffee extract
3 tablespoons coffee liqueur
24–30 chocolate-covered espresso beans for garnish, optional

A day or several hours before serving, prepare Caramel Sauce and chill before using as a glaze.

Preheat oven to 425°F. Prepare Sweet Choux Pastry. Pipe onto lined baking sheets according to "Piping Size How-To" for small choux (page 19). Brush each choux lightly with egg wash and bake for 20 to 25 minutes, or until puffed and golden brown. Turn off the oven, open the door, and let the pastry stand for 5 minutes. Remove choux to a cooling rack, and pierce the bottom of each gently with the tip of a knife. Let cool completely.

To prepare the buttercream, in a large bowl, combine the butter, powdered sugar, salt, and cream cheese with a mixer on low speed, scraping down the sides and bottom with a spatula. When smooth, add the coffee extract and liqueur.

Fill a pastry bag fitted with a #802 round tip with the buttercream. It should be firm but not melting. If the buttercream is too soft, set the filled bag in the refrigerator for 15 to 20 minutes. Pipe about 1 teaspoon into the hole at the bottom of each puff, or a little more to make them expand slightly. Using 1/4 cup of the reserved caramel sauce, glaze each choux with a thin coating of the thickened sauce (now glaze), using a clean fingertip or the back of a teaspoon. Top each with an espresso bean, if desired. Refrigerate for at least 1 hour before serving.

Suggested sauce pairing: These would be excellent with a few tablespoons of the remaining caramel sauce, gently reheated and served on a plate alongside the cream puffs.

GÂTEAU ST. HONORÉ
St. Honoré Cake
(SERVES 8 TO 10)

St. Honoré, arguably one of the loveliest streets in Paris, shares its name with this magnificent cake. The inspiration for both is the patron saint of pastry chefs, Saint Honoré. Appropriately named, this beautiful creation layers pastry, upon pastry, upon pastry and is filled with a pastry cream lightened with whipped cream and topped with more whipped cream for good measure. It is also, frankly, a lot of work.

I've taken a couple steps to make the job easier for you. For example, for the pastry base (which uses puff pastry), we're using commercially prepared pastry. I recommend Pepperidge Farm for its good quality and availability; but substitute as needed. Also, rather than take another step to whip meringue, which is typically folded into the pastry cream base to form a chiboust, *this recipe uses whipped cream to lighten the pastry cream and top the cake. Finally, the whipped cream is traditionally piped onto the top using a round star tip, but in this recipe, we just arrange it prettily on top with a spatula. Making the pastry cream a day ahead lightens the load on St. Honoré assembly day. This is the perfect cake for a special celebration. It's best to fill it and serve it, chilled, within a few hours of assembling.*

It begins with a circular puff pastry base that is ringed with a circle of choux. Once baked, several cream puffs are dipped in warm caramel and adhered to the puff pastry ring. It is a towering master of choux filled with pastry cream and cream—the consummate cream puff!

1 Master Recipe Pastry Cream (page 66)
1 sheet thawed Pepperidge Farm Puff Pastry
1 Master Recipe Sweet Choux Pastry (page 62
Egg wash: 1 egg yolk, splash of water, pinch of salt,
    blended together

For the whipped cream:
1¹/₂ cups very cold whipping cream

¹/₄ cup powdered sugar
1 teaspoon vanilla extract

For the caramel:
¹/₂ cup sugar
2 tablespoons water
¹/₄ cup sifted powdered sugar for garnish

Prepare the Pastry Cream according to directions several hours in advance or 1 day ahead. Keep refrigerated with plastic wrap pressed down on the top to prevent the formation of a "skin."

The day of cake assembly, thaw the puff pastry sheet according to package directions. Preheat oven to 425°F. Line two half-sheet baking pans with silicone mats or parchment paper.

Arrange the thawed pastry sheet on one of the lined baking pans. Trim off the hard corners using a paring knife to form crescent-shaped circles at each corner.

Prepare choux pastry according to directions. Fit a pastry bag with a #804 tip. To form the choux ring base, brush the prepared puff pastry with the egg wash. Pipe the warm dough, using about one-third of the total recipe, along the edges of the puff pastry ring. Pipe the width about $^{1}/_{2}$ inch, as you would for a petite éclair, piping evenly along the circumference of the circle. Leave a $^{1}/_{4}$-inch border between the edge of the puff pastry base and the choux ring so it has room to expand as it bakes. Brush the choux ring lightly with egg wash.

Pipe the remaining warm dough onto the other lined baking sheet according to directions for small choux (page 19). Brush the choux lightly with the remaining egg wash. Place both sheets in the oven and bake for 25 minutes. Remove the petits choux and cool on a pastry rack. Pierce the bottom of each gently with the tip of a knife. Reduce the heat to 375°F. and continue baking the pastry base and choux ring another 10 minutes, until golden brown. Remove from oven and cool completely.

Meanwhile, combine the whipping cream, powdered sugar and vanilla extract in a large bowl. Using a whisk or hand-held blender, beat until very firm, about 3 minutes with a blender, a little longer with a whisk. Whisk 1 cup of the whipped cream into the reserved cold pastry cream. Refrigerate both the whipped cream and the pastry cream mixture in separate bowls.

Fill a pastry bag fitted with a #802 round tip with 1 cup of the reserved pastry cream mixture. Pipe about 1 teaspoon of the cream into the bottom of each choux to form cream puffs. (*Note:* You will need only about 16–18 to cover the perimeter of the pastry ring. Save the remaining unfilled choux for another use, or freeze). Refrigerate the filled choux while you prepare the caramel. Also at this time, transfer the cooled pastry base to a cake plate or serving platter before assembling.

In a small saucepan with high sides, combine the sugar and water by swirling. Heat over high heat for 2 minutes, or until the sugar dissolves. Reduce the heat to medium-high and continue cooking the sugar mixture until it becomes nutty brown and caramelized, an additional 6 to 7 minutes. Very carefully pour the hot (and dangerous!) caramel into a small ramekin (the deeper, smaller space will prevent it from cooling and setting up too quickly). Holding a filled cream puff with tongs, dip the bottom into the warm caramel. Gently press the caramel end on top of the raised choux ring of the cake. Repeat with the remaining puffs, working quickly one by one, as the caramel hardens as it cools. Place puffs all the way around the entire ring, spacing tightly and neatly. If there is any caramel remaining, dip a spoon into it and drizzle it over the choux balls to form pretty cooked sugar strings. (If it's getting hard and is no longer viscous, pop it into the microwave for just a few seconds to reheat.)

Once the caramel has hardened, it's time to fill the cake. Fill the center with the pastry cream mixture and spread evenly with a spatula. Top this with the remaining whipped cream, spreading evenly to meet the corners and edges. Sift the powdered sugar over the edges of the cake to finish. Refrigerate until serving, within the next few hours.

CROQUEMBOUCHE
Crunchy Choux Pyramid Cake

(MAKES 4 INDIVIDUAL CAKES)

Croquembouche are cakes made for celebrations in France, especially weddings. Typically, they are towering pyramids composed of cream puffs filled with whipped cream or pastry cream and held together with caramel. The caramel gives the cream puffs "crunch," hence the name croquembouche, *which means to "crunch in the mouth." A wonderful composed cake, it does present some assembly challenges for its typical form. The higher the cake gets, the more likely it is to topple. And, as the caramel cools in the assembly process, it loses its stick factor. So to keep things simple, this recipe calls for "baby" croquembouche composed of just six cream puffs, three on the bottom, followed by a layer of two, and topped with just one. They are perfectly adorable and very easy to put together. And taking them apart is literally a snap. I love the idea of serving these at the end of a dinner party and letting couples share their cake. Eating them is as much fun as tearing the cream puffs off the cake.*

1 Master Recipe Pastry Cream (page 66)

1 Master Recipe Sweet Choux Pastry (page 62)

Egg wash: 1 egg yolk, splash of water, pinch of salt,
   blended together

1 cup sugar

3 tablespoons water

Several hours or a day before, prepare the Pastry Cream and refrigerate until completely cold. Cover tightly with plastic wrap, pressing it down on the top of the custard to prevent the formation of a skin.

Preheat oven to 425°F.

Prepare the Sweet Choux Pastry. Pipe onto lined baking sheets according to "Piping Size How-To" for small choux (page 19). Brush the puffs lightly with the egg wash. Bake for 20 to 25 minutes, or until puffed and golden brown. Turn off the oven, open the door, and let the pastry stand for 5 minutes. Remove choux to a cooling rack, and when cool enough to handle, pierce the bottom of each gently with the tip of a knife. Let cool completely.

Using a pastry bag fitted with a round #802 tip, fill each cream puff until just full. (*Note:* For easier assembly of the cakes, it is better to just under-fill the cream puffs. You want to avoid custard oozing from the bottom, as it might muddle the caramel). Set the filled cream puffs in the refrigerator to chill completely.

In a small saucepan with high sides, swirl the sugar and water to combine. Set over high heat and swirl a couple more times; let heat for 2 minutes, or until the sugar dissolves. Reduce the heat to medium-high and continue cooking until it becomes nutty brown and caramelized, an additional 6 to 7 minutes. Very carefully pour the hot (and dangerous!) caramel into a medium ramekin (the deeper, smaller space will keep it from cooling too quickly and turning hard).

To form the bottom layer, carefully dip the side of a filled cream puff into the hot caramel. (*Note:* I suggest piercing the top of the puffs with a very small knife and "dipping" it into the caramel, rather than using your fingers). Press the caramel-dipped side gently against a second filled cream puff. Repeat the dipping and pressing with a third puff, to form a tight circle of three cream puffs to form the base.

To form the second layer, dip the bottom of a cream puff into the hot caramel. Press onto the top of the choux base, repeating with a second cream puff.

To form the top layer, dip the bottom of a single filled cream puff into the caramel and

adhere it to the top of the two puffs on the second layer, to form a mini pyramid. Work one by one and quickly, as the caramel hardens quickly. (If it's getting hard and is no longer viscous, pop it into the microwave for just a few seconds to reheat.) Using a spoon, drizzle any remaining caramel over the cakes once they're assembled, to form pretty cooked sugar strings.

Refrigerate until serving. The croquembouche are best served within 4 hours of assembling.

PARIS-BREST
Choux Pastry with Praline-Flavored Cream

(YIELDS 8 TO 10 GENEROUS PORTIONS)

Named after the celebrated annual bicycle race that has been run between these two cities in northern France since the cake was created to commemorate the race's debut in 1891, the ring cake is intended to resemble the round wheels of a bike. It is filled with a rich praline cream, redolent with the buttery, nutty flavor of caramel and toasted pecans. It can be prepared with small rings (page 19), but the large ring makes for a dramatic presentation at celebrations and parties.

1¹/₂ cups pecan halves

1 cup sugar

3 tablespoons water

8 tablespoons (1 stick) unsalted butter, cut into
   small cubes

5 egg yolks

3 tablespoons cornstarch

Generous pinch of salt

2 cups milk

1 teaspoon vanilla extract

1 Master Recipe Sweet Choux Pastry (page 62)

Egg wash: 1 egg yolk, splash of water, pinch of salt,
   blended together

¹/₂ cup powdered sugar

Prepare the praline cream 1 to 2 days before assembling the cake. Begin by toasting the pecan halves in a medium-size sauté pan over medium-high heat, tossing every 30 seconds or so. Once nutty and golden, remove nuts from the pan. When cool enough to handle, chop until fine with a chef's knife. Set aside.

In a medium saucepan with high sides, combine sugar and water by swirling. Set over high heat and swirl a couple more times to combine, then heat for 2 minutes, or until the sugar dissolves. Reduce to medium-high heat and continue cooking until it becomes nutty brown and caramelized, an additional 6 to 7 minutes. Carefully whisk in the butter until it melts and the sauce becomes thick. Reserve warm nearby.

In a medium saucepan, whisk together the egg yolks, cornstarch and salt until lemony in color and thickened. Whisk in the milk in a steady stream. Cook over medium heat, whisking constantly, until it thickens to the consistency of half-mounted whipped cream. Whisk in the reserved warm caramel and continue cooking, whisking, another 5 minutes, or until it has thickened to pudding consistency. Stir in the reserved toasted pecans and the vanilla. Refrigerate, tightly covered with plastic wrap to prevent a skin from forming, for at least 3 hours or overnight.

On the day of assembly and service, prepare the choux ring. Preheat the oven to 425°F. Line one half-sheet baking pan with silicone mats or parchment paper.

Prepare the Sweet Choux Pastry. Pipe a large ring according to "Piping Size How-To" directions for piping large rings (page 19). Brush lightly with egg wash. Bake for 25 minutes, until well puffed and very pale brown. Decrease the heat to 375°F. and bake an additional 10 to 15 minutes, or until the ring is golden brown and firm to the touch. Turn off the oven and allow the ring to "cook" in the oven another 5 minutes. Remove from the oven to a cooling rack. When completely cool to the touch, cut through the ring horizontally using a serrated knife. Be careful to cut evenly and gently, without cutting through the bottom or top of the pastry. Take your time and guide the knife carefully as you work your way around the ring. Remove the lid and set aside. Place the bottom of the ring on the platter or cake stand from which you will be serving.

Using a pastry bag fitted with a large, fluted #867 round tip, pipe the chilled praline cream onto the bottom of the choux ring in a generous ¾-inch layer. You will have just enough to fill the entire cake. Top the ring with its lid. Dust lightly with sifted powdered sugar to garnish. Refrigerate several hours before serving. Cut into 3-inch-wide slices to serve.

LES PROFITEROLES

No French bistro menu or special warm summer evening would be fully complete without the sweet ending of a profiterole. In their truest form, profiteroles are small cream puffs filled with fresh vanilla ice cream, usually served in threes and topped with a rich hot chocolate sauce. A spoon effortlessly breaks through the tender choux to a middle layer of ice cream melting into the sauce with just about every bite. Of course, the cream puffs can be filled with whipped cream or pastry cream, as well, and served with various ice cream and sauce flavors. Pastry or whipped creams can be piped into the center, but I like to see the filling as it meets the sauce and thus suggest cutting the puffs in half for filling. Profiteroles make especially nice do-ahead desserts, as they can be filled and left in the freezer for an hour or two before serving. Remember to take them out about 15 minutes in advance to soften.

HOT TIPS FOR ICE CREAM

Today's world is filled with many first-class commercially prepared ice cream brands, but making your own is truly rewarding and simple. If you don't own an ice cream maker, it's worth the purchase. My Krups basic ice cream machine cost less than $50, lasted 20 years and made countless batches of ice cream. It is possible to make ice cream without an ice cream maker by stirring the blend with a fork every 15 minutes as it is setting up, but the results will be less creamy and less aerated. Most commercial ice cream makers designed for home kitchens use a frozen 1.5-quart container that turns while a paddle moves through the ice cream base to aid in even freezing.

Ice cream in French cooking is a frozen Crème Anglaise (page 114) for vanilla; additional flavorings can be added as outlined in the recipes that follow. A couple of tips to keep in mind:

1. Make the Crème Anglaise the day before and refrigerate overnight. It needs to be cold when it goes into the machine to prevent crystals from forming.

2. Freeze the ice cream maker's canister overnight, as well, for the same reasons. Shake it to test that the internal freezing agent is solid and not sloshing around. If you take these two steps, you will be rewarded with creamy, smooth ice cream in just 20 to 25 minutes.

3. Turn the prepared ice cream out into a well-chilled glass bowl or container, cover tightly, and store in the freezer until ready to use. It should store well for a week.

Profiteroles Classiques avec Glace à la Vanille et Sauce au Chocolat Chaud

Classic Profiteroles with Vanilla Ice Cream and Hot Chocolate Sauce

(YIELDS 8 SERVINGS, 3 CREAM PUFFS PER PERSON)

Classic for a reason: nothing really beats hot chocolate melting over cold, homemade vanilla ice cream.

1 Master Recipe Sweet Choux Pastry (page 62)   Ganache/Hot Chocolate Sauce (page 113)
Crème Anglaise (page 114)

Preheat oven to 425°F.

Prepare Sweet Choux Pastry. Pipe onto lined baking sheets according to "Piping Size How-To" for small choux (page 19). Brush each choux lightly with egg wash and bake for 20 to 25 minutes, or until puffed and golden brown. Turn off the oven, open the door, and let the pastry stand for 5 minutes. Remove choux to a cooling rack, and pierce the bottom of each gently with the tip of a knife. Let cool completely.

A day before freezing, prepare the Crème Anglaise as directed. Chill overnight before freezing in an ice cream freezer. Freeze according to machine directions.

Prepare Ganache/Hot Chocolate Sauce as directed.

To serve, fill each halved cream puff with 2 teaspoons of ice cream, arrange 3 on a plate or shallow bowl, dress with several tablespoons of the warm (not scorching hot) sauce and serve immediately.

Variation: The vanilla ice cream also pairs well with Caramel Sauce (page 118).

Profiteroles avec Glacé au Pistache et Sauce au Chocolat Chaud
Profiteroles with Pistachio Ice Cream and Hot Chocolate Sauce

(YIELDS 8 SERVINGS, 3 CREAM PUFFS PER PERSON)

Pistachios and chocolate are another match made in heaven. A bit of salt on the roasted nuts plays nicely with the sweetness of the ice cream and sauce. The contrast of pale green with dark chocolate is also lovely. If you like, add a tiny pinch of green food coloring to the ice cream base; but I prefer it "au natural."

1 Master Recipe Sweet Choux Pastry (page 62)
Crème Anglaise (page 114)
$^1/_2$ cup coarsely chopped roasted salted pistachios

$^1/_2$ teaspoon almond extract
Ganache/Hot Chocolate Sauce (page 113)

Preheat oven to 425°F.

Prepare Sweet Choux Pastry. Pipe onto lined baking sheets according to "Piping Size How-To" for small choux (page 19). Brush each choux lightly with egg wash and bake for 20 to 25 minutes, or until puffed and golden brown. Turn off the oven, open the door, and let the pastry stand for 5 minutes. Remove choux to a cooling rack, and pierce the bottom of each gently with the tip of a knife. Let cool completely.

A day before freezing, prepare the Crème Anglaise as directed, minus the vanilla pod, vanilla extract and salt. Chill overnight before freezing in an ice cream freezer.

Freeze according to machine directions, adding pistachios and almond extract 10 minutes into the freezing process, before the ice cream is fully set. Continue freezing until set, about 15 more minutes.

Prepare Ganache/Hot Chocolate Sauce as directed.

To serve, fill each halved cream puff with 2 teaspoons of ice cream, arrange 3 on a plate or shallow bowl, dress with several tablespoons of the warm (not scorching hot) sauce and serve immediately.

Profiteroles avec Glace de Caramel Salé aux Noix de Macadamia et Sauce au Caramel Chaud

Profiteroles with Salted Caramel Macadamia Nut Ice Cream and Warm Caramel Sauce

(YIELDS 8 SERVINGS, 3 CREAM PUFFS PER PERSON)

Caramel lovers will think they've died and gone to France with this heady combination of caramel and crunch macadamia nut ice cream with hot caramel sauce.

1 Master Recipe Sweet Choux Pastry (page 62)
Crème Anglaise (page 114)
Caramel Sauce (page 118)

$^1/_4$ teaspoon sea salt or kosher salt
$^1/_2$ cup coarsely chopped, salted macadamia nuts

Preheat oven to 425°F.

Prepare Sweet Choux Pastry. Pipe onto lined baking sheets according to "Piping Size How-To" for small choux (page 19). Brush each choux lightly with egg wash and bake for 20 to 25 minutes, or until puffed and golden brown. Turn off the oven, open the door, and let the pastry stand for 5 minutes. Remove choux to a cooling rack, and pierce the bottom of each gently with the tip of a knife. Let cool completely.

A day before freezing, prepare the Caramel Sauce and Crème Anglaise. Cover and refrigerate each separately overnight.

The next day, whisk $^1/_3$ cup plus 1 tablespoon cooled Caramel Sauce and salt into the chilled Crème Anglaise base. Freeze according to package directions, adding nuts 10 minutes into the freezing process, before the ice cream is fully set. Continue freezing until set, about 15 more minutes. Warm the remaining prepared caramel sauce over medium-low heat.

To serve, fill each halved cream puff with 2 teaspoons of ice cream, arrange 3 on a plate or shallow bowl, dress with several tablespoons of the warm (not scorching hot) sauce and serve immediately.

Beignets aux Coulis aux Framboises
Beignets with Raspberry Coulis

(YIELDS 12 BEIGNETS)

Beignets are French doughnuts prepared by frying choux in hot oil. The dough puffs up while it cooks, making it even more light and airy, and the frying gives it an appealing exterior crust and color. Dusted with some powdered sugar fresh out of the fryer and served warm in a pool of a cool, fresh raspberry sauce, there is practically nothing finer. Do use a high-temperature smoke point, flavorless oil such as canola, peanut, or vegetable. Have paper towels nearby for draining after the beignets come out of the fryer. These are perfect fare for a celebratory weekend brunch.

Raspberry Sauce (page 117)
1 Master Recipe Sweet Choux Pastry (page 62)

6 cups vegetable, peanut or canola oil
$1/2$ cup powdered sugar

Several hours ahead or the day before, prepare the raspberry sauce. Cover and refrigerate until ready to use.

Prepare the Sweet Choux Pastry as directed. Reserve the uncooked choux in the bowl while the oil heats. Pour the oil into a high-sided 2-quart saucepan. Heat over medium-high until the oil starts to slither and swirl along the bottom of the pan and begins to make popping noises. This will take about 5 minutes.

The ideal temperature for deep-frying is 300°F. (I recommend using a thermometer.) When the oil is hot, begin cooking the beignets in batches of 4 or 5 at a time. Dip an everyday table service soup spoon into cold water. Fill to heaping with choux. Carefully drop the first "test" beignet from the spoon into the hot oil. It should pop to the surface within 30 seconds. (If it doesn't, the oil isn't hot enough. Wait a few more minutes and try again.) Add 3 or 4 additional beignets to the oil in rapid succession. After 4 or 5 minutes, they will start to puff and expand noticeably. Turn each with a spoon from time to time, to brown and cook evenly. Cook 8 to 10 minutes, total, or until airy and golden brown. Drain on paper towels. Repeat with the remaining beignets. Reserve drained beignets in a warm oven until ready to serve.

Serve the beignets warm, 1 to 2 per plate over a $1/3$-cup pool of the cool sauce. Sprinkle each with a tablespoon or so of powdered sugar. Serve immediately.

CHAPTER 4

LES ÉCLAIRS SUCRÉES
Sweet Éclairs

Typically, éclair fillings are piped into the interiors rather than through an open top, as with some of the cream puffs in the previous chapter. However, I make a few exceptions here, just because the Gimme S'more Éclairs (page 102) interior is a big part of the "melting" show and because the Lime and White Chocolate éclairs (page 101) present piping challenges and have such a lovely, snowy white interior color. In all other recipes, the filling, whether a pastry cream, custard or butter cream, is piped using a small, #802 round pastry tip. Because the bottom surface area is narrower than a cream

puff and also has more piping entry holes, a smaller tip is recommended to prevent messy piping and "oozing" afterwards(see Éclair Piping Clean-Up tips, page 100).

Unlike cream puffs, éclairs are almost never served with a sauce. Once again, the recipes here include a few exceptions. In addition to the flavor pairings that follow, remember a good old-fashioned éclair filled with a simple pastry cream and topped with chocolate ganache is still a universal favorite. Feel free to mix and match for delicious fun all along the way!

PETITS ÉCLAIRS COMME "CANNOLI"
Small "Cannoli" Éclairs
(YIELDS 22 TO 26 PETITS ÉCLAIRS)

Although cannoli typically are considered Italian pastries filled with sweetened ricotta, the wide open flavor canvas of buttery, flaky choux lends itself perfectly to a similar filling. Here, the cute little éclairs are filled with the creamy filling, glazed with a cool ganache and drizzled with chopped pistachio, a la "cannoli." The sturdy filling holds up well with time. These can be prepared and refrigerated for several hours (or, less ideally, overnight) before serving. Make the ganache first or borrow from an already prepared batch.

1 Master Recipe Sweet Choux Pastry (page 62)
Egg wash: 1 egg yolk, splash of water, pinch of salt, blended together

For the filling:
1/2 cup cream cheese, at room temperature
1/2 cup whole ricotta cheese
3 tablespoons heavy cream

Seeds from 1 vanilla bean, cut vertically and seeds removed with the edge of a paring knife
1/3 cup powdered sugar
1/8 teaspoon almond extract

For the garnish:
1/2 cup chilled Ganache/Hot Chocolate Sauce (page 113)
1/4 cup finely chopped, roasted and salted pistachios

Preheat oven to 425°F.

Prepare the Sweet Choux Pastry. Pipe the warm choux according to directions for "Piping Size How-To" for small éclairs (page 19). Brush each lightly with egg wash and bake for 20 to 25 minutes, or until puffed and golden. Turn off the oven, open the door, and let the pastry stand for 5 minutes. Remove éclairs to a cooling rack, and pierce the bottom of each gently with a knife twice, once near each end of the length of the éclairs.

To prepare the filling, in a large bowl, combine all of the filling ingredients with an electric blender on medium speed until aerated and smooth, about 2 minutes, scraping down the sides and bottom with a spatula as you go. Using a pastry bag fitted with a #802 round pastry tip, gently pipe the filling into each of the two knife piercings on the bottom of each éclair.

Prepare the Ganache/Hot Chocolate Sauce and let cool. Using a clean fingertip or the back of a teaspoon, spread a heaping teaspoon of Ganache evenly over the top of each éclair. Garnish with a sprinkling of the chopped pistachios. Serve cold. These are excellent with hot coffee for dessert or as a breakfast pastry. They also make excellent party fare!

Gros Éclairs à la Crème de Myrtilles et Citron, Glaçage au Chocolat

Large Éclairs with Lemon Blueberry Cream and Chocolate Glaze

(YIELDS 12 TO 16 GROS ÉCLAIRS)

A purée of fresh blueberries blended into a rich pastry cream give the filling for these beauties a regal purple color. The mild flavor of the berries is lightly enhanced with fresh lemon juice. Fresh, sugar-coated berries sit atop a ganache glaze to provide an enticing clue as to what's inside. You could easily substitute the same quantity of fresh raspberries or blackberries using the same method for a color and flavor variation. Just switch out the garnish to match the corresponding berry-enriched filling. Make the pastry cream and the ganache ahead, so they can chill and set up, or borrow from a previously prepared batch. These will chill nicely for several hours before serving. They are superb with a cold glass of Champagne or sparkling wine garnished with 3 or 4 fresh, frozen blueberries to serve as edible ice cubes.

1 Master Recipe Sweet Choux Pastry (page 62)

Egg wash: 1 egg yolk, splash of water, pinch of salt, blended together

3 tablespoons water

Pinch of sea salt or kosher salt

2 cups prepared, cold Pastry Cream (page 66)

For the filling:

2 cups fresh blueberries

1/4 cup sugar

Zest of 1 lemon

Juice of 1 lemon

For the garnish:

1/2 cup Ganache/Hot Chocolate Sauce (page 113), cold

1/4 cup dampened fresh blueberries

2 tablespoons sugar

Preheat oven to 425°F.

Prepare the Sweet Choux Pastry. Pipe the warm choux according to directions for "Piping Size How-To" for large éclairs (page 19). Brush lightly with the egg wash. Bake 25 minutes. Reduce heat to 375F, rotating the sheets if necessary for even browning, and bake another 10 minutes. Remove from the oven and cool on a pastry rack. Pierce the bottom of each gently with the tip of a sharp knife three times, once near each end of the length of the éclairs and once in the center.

Prepare the filling. In a medium saucepan, bring the blueberries, sugar, lemon zest, lemon juice, water and salt up to a simmer over high heat. Reduce to medium. Cook until the blueberries

continued >

begin to pop and soften, stirring occasionally, a total of about 6 to 7 minutes. Using a blender or a hand-held emulsion blender, purée the mixture until very smooth. Return the mixture to the same pan, bring to a boil, and reduce to a simmer until thickened and reduced to a total of 1 cup. Refrigerate until the mixture is thoroughly chilled.

In a medium bowl, whisk together the pastry cream with the blueberry sauce ("coulis") until smooth and blended. Using a pastry bag fitted with a #802 round pastry tip, gently pipe the filling into each of the three knife piercings on the bottom of each éclair. Using a clean fingertip, garnish the top of each with a heaping tablespoon of ganache spread out into a smooth layer over the top of the éclair. Just before garnishing, run the reserved $1/4$ cup blueberries under water and strain well. Toss with the sugar. Garnish the top of each éclair with a horizontal string of 5 blueberries along the top, pressed gently into the ganache.

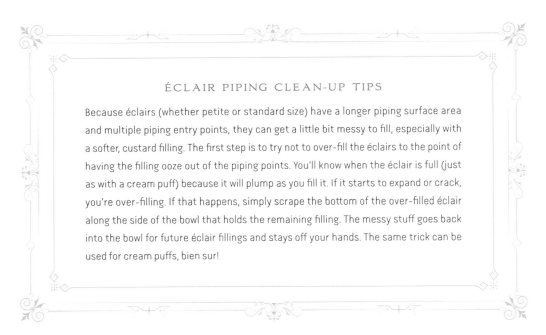

ÉCLAIR PIPING CLEAN-UP TIPS

Because éclairs (whether petite or standard size) have a longer piping surface area and multiple piping entry points, they can get a little bit messy to fill, especially with a softer, custard filling. The first step is to try not to over-fill the éclairs to the point of having the filling ooze out of the piping points. You'll know when the éclair is full (just as with a cream puff) because it will plump as you fill it. If it starts to expand or crack, you're over-filling. If that happens, simply scrape the bottom of the over-filled éclair along the side of the bowl that holds the remaining filling. The messy stuff goes back into the bowl for future éclair fillings and stays off your hands. The same trick can be used for cream puffs, bien sur!

Petits Éclairs à la Crème de Citron Vert et Chocolat Blanc
Small Éclairs with a Lime and White Chocolate Cream

(YIELDS 22 TO 26 PETITS ÉCLAIRS)

The snow-white whipped cream filling is flecked with bits of lime green zest and amped with fresh lime flavor in these little éclairs. Finely chopped white chocolate is folded in for a just-right flavor and texture finish. Because the chocolate has a tendency to clump in the cream and clog the pastry tip, it's better to cut the éclairs in half and plop some of the delicious, delicate filling in the center, smoothing to finish with a spoon or spatula. A dusting of powdered sugar continues the snowy effect. Delicious as is, these would also be lovely with a small pool of hot chocolate sauce (page 113) or add a tablespoon of cocoa powder to the powdered sugar garnish for a chocolate edge that plays so well with lime. Keep very cold before serving and serve within an hour or two. The whipped cream filling is not as stable as a pastry cream or a butter cream, but it is oh so good!

1 Master Recipe Sweet Choux Pastry (page 62)

Egg wash: 1 egg yolk, splash of water, pinch of salt, blended together

For the filling:
Zest of 3 limes, finely chopped
Juice of 3 limes (about $^1/_3$ cup)

1 cup very cold whipping cream

$^1/_4$ cup powdered sugar

4 ounces best-quality white chocolate (suggest Ghirardelli brand), very finely chopped

For the garnish:
$^1/_2$ cup powdered sugar

Preheat oven to 425°F.

Prepare the Sweet Choux Pastry. Pipe the warm choux according to directions for "Piping Size How-To" petits éclairs, (page 19). Brush lightly with the egg wash. Bake for 22 to 25 minutes, or until puffed and golden. Remove from the oven and cool on a pastry rack. Pierce the bottom of each gently with the tip of a sharp knife twice, once near each end of the length of the éclairs.

To prepare the filling, combine the lime zest and lime juice in a small saucepan. Bring to a boil over high heat and cook, 2 to 3 minutes, or until the liquid has reduced down to just 1 tablespoon. Pour it out into a small ramekin and refrigerate until completely cool.

In a medium bowl, whip the cold cream with the $^1/_4$ cup powdered sugar until firm, using an electric mixer, about 3 minutes. Fold in the lime juice/zest reduction and the white chocolate.

Cut the éclairs in half horizontally with a serrated knife, stopping just before cutting all the way through. Plop a generous teaspoon of the filling into each and cap lightly with its top. Dust each éclair with powdered sugar. Chill in the freezer for 15 minutes before serving.

Gros Éclairs de Beurre de Cacahuètes, Pâte de Guimauve et Chocolat

Gimme S'more Éclairs

(YIELDS 12 TO 16 GROS ÉCLAIRS)

Just as in the United States, French kids of all ages love to sit around camp fires and hearths, melting marshmallows and sandwiching them between crackers and chocolate for a makeshift S'more. So, why not sandwich the same fillings between an éclair? These are so much fun to make, especially with and for children. I add peanut butter, too, because I love the flavor with chocolate and marshmallow. These éclairs are left "open" to reveal the warm, oozing marshmallow and chocolate interior. The marshmallow can be toasted either using a blow torch or by broiling for a few minutes under a hot broiler. Serve them while still warm.

1 Master Recipe Sweet Choux Pastry (page 62)
1 egg wash—yolk, splash water, pinch salt, mixed
    together

For the filling:

1 cup creamy peanut butter
1 cup marshmallow fluff
1 cup semi-sweet miniature chocolate chips
$1/2$ cup powdered sugar for garnish

Preheat oven to 425°F.

Prepare the Sweet Choux Pastry. Pipe the warm choux according to directions for "Piping Size How-To" for large éclairs (page 19). Brush lightly with the egg wash. Bake 25 minutes. Reduce heat to 375°F, rotating the sheets if necessary for even browning, and bake another 10 minutes. Remove from the oven and cool on a pastry rack. Pierce the bottom of each gently with the tip of a sharp knife three times, once near each end of the length of the éclairs and once in the center.

Once cool, using a serrated knife, cut all the way through each éclair horizontally along its length (reserving the tops separately). To assemble, spread 1 generous tablespoon of peanut butter on the bottom of each, spreading evenly with a spatula or a spoon. Top this with another generous tablespoon of marshmallow fluff and spread evenly. To brown/warm the marshmallow, torch with a kitchen blow torch until evenly browned or bubbling, or arrange on a baking sheet under a hot broiler until brown and bubbling. Carefully, evenly scatter a heaping tablespoon of the chocolate chips over the warm marshmallow. Top each éclair and serve while still warm. Dust powdered sugar evenly over the top of each to garnish.

For extra chocolate fun, serve these with a few tablespoons of Hot Chocolate Sauce (page 113).

Gros Éclairs à la Crème Pâtissière de Banane aux Noix de Macadamia, Glaçage au Caramel

Large Éclairs with Banana Cream, Macadamia Nuts and Caramel Glaze

(YIELDS 12 TO 16 GROS ÉCLAIRS)

Do you want to hear a confession? Voici! This is one of my favorite recipes in this book, and perhaps one of my favorite recipes ever. How could it not be delicious? Rich, unctuous pastry cream is blended with fresh, mashed bananas, the éclair is glazed with a nutty, fragrant caramel sauce and salty, crunchy macadamia nuts go on top. Select bananas that are ripe and fragrant but not spotted or overripe. If the pastry cream, caramel sauce and éclairs are prepared a day ahead, they come together in minutes. They will keep cold for several hours before serving.

1 Master Recipe Sweet Choux Pastry (page 62)

1 egg wash—yolk, splash water, pinch salt, mixed together

1 Master Recipe Pastry Cream (page 66), cold

2 ripe bananas, mashed (about ²/₃ cup)

¹/₂ recipe Caramel Sauce (page 118), cold

¹/₂ cup finely chopped, salted roasted macadamia nuts

Preheat oven to 425°F. Prepare the Sweet Choux Pastry. Pipe the warm choux according to directions for "Piping Size How-To" for large éclairs (page 19). Brush lightly with the egg wash. Bake 25 minutes. Reduce heat to 375°F, rotating the sheets if necessary for even browning, and bake another 10 minutes. Remove from the oven and cool on a pastry rack. Pierce the bottom of each gently with the tip of a sharp knife three times, once near each end of the length of the éclairs and once in the center.

Prepare the Pastry Cream as directed. Chill for at least 3 hours, tightly covered with plastic wrap pressed down over the top surface to prevent a skin from forming.

Meanwhile, prepare the Caramel Sauce and refrigerate 2 to 3 hours, or until firm. Just before filling the éclairs, peel and mash the bananas until smooth. Fold the mashed bananas into the pastry cream. Using a pastry bag fitted with a #802 round pastry tip, gently pipe the filling into each of the three knife piercings on the bottom of each éclair. Using a clean fingertip or the back of a teaspoon, glaze the full length of the top of each éclair with the cooled caramel sauce, about 2 tablespoons per éclair. Top each with a dusting of the chopped nuts. Press the nuts lightly into the caramel to help them stick.

Petits Éclairs à la Crème de Fraise Façon de "Shortcake"

Small Strawberry Cream "Shortcake" Éclairs

(YIELDS 22 TO 26 PETITS ÉCLAIRS)

Strawberries and cream are a dream team in so many classic desserts, including strawberry shortcake. In this recipe, the éclair is the "shortcake" and the cream is a blend of unsalted butter, cream cheese and a luscious fresh strawberry purée. The results are simply stunning, especially when using summer's sweetest berries. A fresh strawberry royal icing forms the glaze. If desired, finely chop basil and sprinkle over the top for a splash of color as well as the bright flavor of basil that pairs so well with strawberries. These were good enough to make my neighbor's young daughters, Margaret and Elizabeth, declare "You're a good cooker, Miss Holly," even as they rubbed their little bellies in glee. Your friends and children will do the same.

1 Master Recipe Sweet Choux Pastry (page 62)

Egg wash: 1 egg yolk, splash of water, pinch of salt, blended together

For the filling:

1¹/₂ cups fresh strawberries, rinsed, trimmed and cut in half

1 tablespoon strawberry jam

2 sticks (1 cup) unsalted butter, room temperature

1 cup cream cheese, room temperature

2 cups powdered sugar

1 teaspoon vanilla extract

Pinch of salt

For the royal icing:

¹/₂ cup powdered sugar

1 tablespoon reserved strawberry purée

Garnish:

¹/₄ cup thinly sliced fresh strawberries

2 tablespoons finely chopped fresh basil

Preheat oven to 425°F. Prepare the Sweet Choux Pastry. Pipe the warm choux according to directions for "Piping Size How-To" for small éclairs (page 19). Brush lightly with the egg wash. Bake for 20 to 25 minutes, or until golden brown. Turn off the oven, open the door, and let the pastry stand for 5 minutes. Remove éclairs to a cooling rack, and pierce the bottom of each gently with a knife twice, once near each end of the length of the éclairs.

In the bowl of a food processor fitted with a metal blade or in a blender, purée the strawberries and the preserves together until very smooth, 1 to 2 minutes, scraping down the sides and the bottom to loosen any strawberry chunks.

In a large bowl, beat together the butter and the cream cheese with an electric mixer at medium speed until very smooth, scraping down the sides and bottom a couple of times. Incorporate the 2 cups powdered sugar in two parts, using low to medium speed, until aerated and fluffy.

Mix in the strawberry purée (reserving 1 tablespoon for the royal icing), vanilla and pinch of salt until fully incorporated.

Using a pastry bag fitted with a #802 round pastry tip, gently pipe the filling into each of the two knife piercings on the bottom of each éclair. Chill for 15 to 20 minutes.

In a small bowl, combine the powdered sugar with the reserved tablespoon of strawberry purée until smooth. Using a clean fingertip or the back of a teaspoon, dress the éclairs with a royal icing glaze along the top and full length of each one. If desired, garnish each with one or two slices of fresh strawberry halves and a light sprinkle of fresh basil leaves.

Gros Éclairs Exotiques à la Crème Pâtissière d'Mandarine et Anana

Large Éclairs with an Exotic Mandarin Orange and Pineapple Cream

(YIELDS 12 TO 16 GROS ÉCLAIRS)

It's so tropical and sweet, you can practically imagine yourself swinging in a hammock somewhere in the French Caribbean with every creamy, fruity bite. Pastry cream is fortified with butter and finished with a reduction of mandarin oranges and pineapple. Chocolate ganache and more fresh pineapple on top seal the garnish deal. Make the pastry cream just before preparing the fruit reduction, as it will need to be warm to blend in the butter. Prepare the ganache the day before you put this together for quick, easy work.

1 Master Recipe Sweet Choux Pastry (page 62)

Egg wash: 1 egg yolk, splash of water, pinch of salt, blended together

For the filling:

1 Master Recipe Pastry Cream (page 66)

1 (11-ounce) can Mandarin orange segments, well drained

1 (6-ounce) can fresh pineapple juice ($^3/_4$ cup)—do not use concentrate!

1 vanilla pod, halved vertically

4 tablespoons unsalted, cold butter, cut into 4 cubes

For the garnish:

$^1/_2$ cup Ganache/Hot Chocolate Sauce (page 113), cold

1 (8-ounce) can crushed pineapple, drained

Preheat oven to 425°F. Prepare the Sweet Choux Pastry. Pipe the warm choux according to directions for "Piping Size How-To" for large éclairs (page 19). Brush lightly with the egg wash. Bake 25 minutes. Reduce heat to 375°F., rotating the sheets if necessary for even browning, and bake another 10 minutes. Remove from the oven and cool on a baking rack. Pierce the bottom of each gently with a knife three times, once near each end of the length of the éclairs and once in the center.

Prepare the Pastry Cream as directed. Reserve warm.

Meanwhile, in a medium saucepan, combine the oranges, pineapple juice and vanilla bean, poking down the bean to make sure it's submerged. Simmer over medium-high until the liquid is reduced to just a glaze, 12 minutes. Remove and discard the vanilla bean. Using a hand-held immersion blender or a countertop blender, purée the mixture until very smooth. Set aside to cool slightly. Whisk the butter, tablespoon by tablespoon, into the warm pastry cream until fully incorporated. Whisk in the reserved cooled fruit purée. Chill completely, at least 2 to 3 hours, covered tightly with plastic wrap pressed against the custard to prevent a skin from forming.

Using a pastry bag fitted with a #802 round pastry tip, gently pipe the filling into each of the three knife piercings in the bottom of each éclair. Chill for 15 to 20 minutes.

Using a clean fingertip or the back of a teaspoon, garnish all along the top of each éclair with the cold Ganache, using about 2 tablespoons for each. Garnish each with a small "line" of fresh pineapple. Refrigerate for up to 5 hours before serving.

CHAPTER 5

LES SAUCES SUCRÉES
Sweet Sauces

In France, sweet cream puffs and éclairs, with the exception of profiteroles (page 87), are rarely served with a sauce. Much like cupcakes, they tend to stand alone perfectly fine with their respective fillings and toppings. However, a little dab of sauce can go a long way in dressing up a plate and adding flavor and a pop of color.

Throughout, I have provided suggestions for which sauces to pair with which cream puffs or éclairs. If you do choose to pair any of them with a sauce, remember to plate the sauce in a small amount (maybe a few tablespoons), so your cream puffs or éclairs aren't swimming. Also, plate them with the sauce just before serving to prevent the delicate choux from getting soggy.

These are beautiful sweet sauces to have in your arsenal, and several of them, such as the Crème Anglaise (page 114), do double duty, in this case as a sauce and a basic ice cream base. More good news: all can be made ahead.

Sauce Crème Sucrée au Vanille
Sweetened Vanilla Cream Sauce

(YIELDS 1¼ CUPS)

Little more than sweetened whipping cream infused with fresh vanilla, this super-easy and delicious sauce should be served cold and in small quantities to add just a bit of saucy creaminess to your choux. Make it a day or several hours ahead to maximize the vanilla flavor. Use any leftovers to flavor your morning coffee, perhaps while enjoying a fresh cream puff.

1 cup heavy whipping cream
3 tablespoons sugar

1 fresh vanilla bean, halved horizontally to expose the seeds (or substitute 1 teaspoon vanilla extract)
Pinch of sea salt or kosher salt

Place all of the ingredients together in a small saucepan. Stir to combine. Bring to a simmer over medium-high heat, then reduce to medium-low. Cook together for about 5 minutes, or until the vanilla has infused the sauce with flavor and aroma. Remove from heat and discard the vanilla bean. Once the sauce has cooled slightly, cover and refrigerate until ready to use. It will store for 2 or 3 days, assuming the cream was very fresh to begin with.

Variations: Stir in 1 to 2 tablespoons of cocoa powder, a bit of citrus zest, or a splash or two of liqueur to suit your taste.

GANACHE
Hot Chocolate Sauce

(YIELDS 1¹/₂ CUPS)

It was a happy day when this relatively recent, easy and versatile sauce/glaze/filling was created. Its function varies, depending on the chocolate-to-cream ratio and whether it is served hot or cold. In its hot state, its viscous, deep dark chocolate color makes a beautiful sauce easily embellished with liqueurs or other flavorings. Cold or at room temperature, ganache works beautifully as a glaze for sweet cream puffs and éclairs. I add a bit of salt along with vanilla and coffee extracts to pump up the chocolate flavor. (Note: You can also make a white chocolate sauce by changing out the dark chocolate for a best-quality white chocolate and removing the coffee extract from the recipe.)

1 cup heavy cream

1 cup coarsely chopped, best-quality dark bittersweet chocolate

Generous pinch of sea salt or kosher salt

¹/₂ teaspoon vanilla extract

¹/₄ teaspoon coffee extract

In a medium saucepan, bring the cream to a simmer over medium-high heat. Reduce heat to low and stir in the chopped dark chocolate. Stir until the chocolate is completely melted and the sauce is a dark color. Remove from the heat and stir in the remaining ingredients. To reserve warm, store in a Thermos, or reheat gently over low heat. To store cold, refrigerate in a covered container for later use as a glaze or reconstituted sauce. For a glaze, remove from the refrigerator for 15 to 20 minutes to soften it for spreading. For a sauce, reheat gently over low heat.

Variations: Stir in suitable liqueurs or extracts, such as hazelnut, coffee, or orange, to taste. Remember, a little bit goes a long way.

CRÈME ANGLAISE
Basic Vanilla Custard Sauce

(YIELDS 2 1/2 CUPS)

This creamy, vanilla-scented custard sauce is widely served as a sauce with many classic French desserts, and it suits just about any sweet cream puff or éclair recipe in this book. It also serves as a base for any and all flavored ice creams (see profiteroles and ice cream, page 87).

It's a snap to make but needs your full attention, mild heat and constant stirring to avoid a panful of sweet scrambled eggs. If it looks like it's starting to curdle or over-thicken, you can rescue it in the final straining process: move it quickly off the heat and strain immediately.

1 cup whole milk	4 egg yolks
1 cup half & half	1/2 cup sugar
1 fresh vanilla bean, halved vertically to	Pinch of sea salt or kosher salt
expose seeds	1 teaspoon vanilla extract

Prepare an ice and water bath in a large bowl by adding a few cups of ice and 1 cup of water. Also, have a chinois or fine strainer nearby in case it is needed to rescue a curdling sauce.

In a large saucepan, heat together the milk, half & half, and vanilla bean over medium heat. Bring to a low simmer.

Separately, combine the egg yolks, sugar and salt in a medium bowl and whisk vigorously until lemony and frothy, about 1 minute. Once the milk mixture is simmering, gradually stream it into the egg mixture, whisking the entire time, until it has all been added. Return the sauce to the same pan the milk was heated in, and cook it over medium-low heat. With a wooden spoon, stir constantly, reaching all edges and bottom of the pan. At first there will be froth on the top of the sauce. This will disappear after 3 minutes. Watch closely and keep stirring another 1 or 2 minutes, until the sauce has thickened slightly and naps the back of the spoon. You will know it is done when you run your finger down the back of the spoon and get a clear strip that holds, without the sauce running back over it, or when a thermometer reaches 170°F.

Pour the sauce through the chinois into a clean bowl. Cool crème anglaise over the water bath to get it to safe temperature and stop the cooking. Stir in the vanilla extract. Cover and refrigerate until ready to use.

COULIS AUX FRAMBOISES
Raspberry Sauce

(YIELDS 2 CUPS)

A coulis is a quickly cooked sauce, frequently made with berries or fruit, that is then puréed to thicken and smooth the sauce. Best served cold, this jewel-hued beauty of a sauce is mildly acidic and as fresh as a berry patch. It can be refrigerated, covered, for a few days before serving.

4 cups (2 pints) fresh raspberries

$^1/_3$ cup sugar

Juice of $^1/_2$ lemon (about 1 tablespoon)

1 tablespoon grenadine syrup

2 tablespoons crème de cassis liqueur, optional

$^1/_4$ cup water

Pinch of sea salt or kosher salt

In a medium saucepan, combine all of the ingredients by stirring with a wooden spoon. Bring to a boil over medium-high heat, and then reduce to a steady simmer, stirring until the berries begin to break up, about 5 minutes. Purée with a blender or food processor until smooth and frothy. The sauce can be covered and refrigerated for up to 3 days.

Variations: Any leftovers are delicious over plain yogurt or as a topping for sliced bananas. It could also be swirled (about $^1/_2$ cup total) into an ice cream base/Crème Anglaise (page 114) to make a beautiful raspberry ice cream and filling for a profiterole (page 87). If you are unable to find crème de cassis, it can be omitted.

Sauce au Caramel
Caramel Sauce

(YIELDS 1¹/₄ CUPS)

Like its sauce cousin ganache, a chilled and hardened caramel sauce can also serve as a delicious glaze for a cream puff or éclair. Or it can flavor a delicious ice cream (see Salted Caramel Macadamia Ice Cream, page 90).

Making caramel sauce—basically cooked and caramelized sugar finished with cream and butter—is not difficult, but the process deserves attention and respect. Hot caramel is dangerously hot stuff. Keep your eyes on it at all times and prepare it when young children and pets are not around. It's best to have everything measured and ready to go before you get started. It takes a few minutes to get there, but once the sugar starts caramelizing, it goes really fast. Your nose will know. Your kitchen will smell faintly of caramel after about 5 or 6 minutes. Once it's a golden, toasted color, it's time to finish it off.

1 cup sugar

3 tablespoons water

4 tablespoons unsalted butter, room temperature, cut into 4 pieces

¹/₂ cup whole cream

¹/₂ teaspoon vanilla extract

Generous pinch of sea salt or kosher salt

In a medium, heavy-bottom saucepan, stir together the sugar and water with a wooden spoon. Cook over low heat, uncovered, until the sugar granules are melted, about 2 minutes. Increase heat to medium-high and allow to simmer vigorously, stirring occasionally (not constantly, or it might crystallize) with a wooden spoon. After 5 to 6 minutes, large bubbles will start forming at the top. This, along with a mild caramel aroma, is your sign that the sugar is about to caramelize. Keep cooking, swishing the pan carefully, but not stirring, until the sugar turns fragrant and a nutty, caramel brown. Remove from the heat. Drop butter carefully into the pan. The caramel will react when the butter hits it by bubbling up aggressively. Proceed with caution to avoid a burn. Whisk the sauce gently to incorporate.

Return the pan to low heat, drizzle in the cream and whisk to incorporate. Simmer for 2 or 3 minutes, whisking to help reincorporate any caramel that has hardened until it becomes a thick and creamy golden sauce. Remove from heat and stir in the vanilla extract and salt. Serve hot or warm.

A CKNOWLEDGMENTS

In addition to all of the artisans and chefs that made French cooking what it is, and particularly the crafty Frenchmen who created wonderful pâte à choux, I am grateful to so many people for the making of this book. Huge gratitude goes to Madge Baird, my wonderful editor whose brainchild this cookbook series is, for believing in me again and for being such a joy to work with. Thank you to the design team—Melissa Dymock and Sheryl Dickert—and photographer Alexandra DeFurio and her team for their talent and beautiful work. Thank you to my agent Joelle Delbourgo for her support, especially on the days when I really needed it.

As with all my books and my life, they really wouldn't be quite the same without my wonderful neighbors, who are my friends and also serve as my recipe taste-testers; their frankness and enthusiasm mean so much. Things got a little heated with this book, especially once I got to the sweet éclairs and cream puffs. On tasting afternoons, I felt like a pied piper of cream puffs, developing a literal following as I passed down the street handing out cream puffs and éclairs.

Finally, thank you to my best friend and stealthy choux thief, my cocker spaniel Tann Mann, who worked faithfully by my side, flashing his beautiful baby browns, throughout the making of this book. *Merci a vous, mes amis, and bon appetit!*

Index

METRIC CONVERSION CHART

Volume Measurements

U.S.	Metric
1 teaspoon	5 ml
1 tablespoon	15 ml
1/4 cup	60 ml
1/3 cup	75 ml
1/2 cup	125 ml
2/3 cup	150 ml
3/4 cup	175 ml
1 cup	250 ml

Weight Measurements

U.S.	Metric
1/2 ounce	15 g
1 ounce	30 g
3 ounces	90 g
4 ounces	115 g
8 ounces	225 g
12 ounces	350 g
1 pound	450 g
2 1/4 pounds	1 kg

Temperature Conversion

Fahrenheit	Celsius
250	120
300	150
325	160
350	180
375	190
400	200
425	220
450	230

Holly Herrick is a recipient of Le Grande Diplome in Pastry and Cuisine, Le Cordon Bleu, Paris, France. Fluent in French and a bonafide Francophile who once called Paris and southern France home, she now resides in Charleston, South Carolina. She is the author of six cookbooks and is underway with her seventh, the third in The French Cook series. A former restaurant critic and multi-awarded food and travel writer, she also enjoys tennis, swimming, visiting farmers markets and long walks around her adopted southern city. Follow her blogs and work at www.hollyherrick.com.